PODCAST REVOLUTION Magazine

PODCAST MONETIZATION TIPS FOR BEGINNERS

CTR MEDIA NETWORK THE NEW STANDARD OF PODCASTING

 **8** PODCAST PRODUCTION TIPS

100 TOP PODCASTERS

MEET THE YOUNGEST PODCASTER IN THE WORLD

THE POWER OF PODCASTING

DR. TINA J. RAMSAY
IN PURSUIT OF A DREAM

PODCAST DIRECTORY & EVENTS INSIDE

TABLE

You will Learn about

- PODCAST MONETIZATION
- WAYS TO STAY MOTIVATED
- 8 PODCAST PRODUCTION TIPS
- PRACTICAL WAYS TO OVERCOME NERVOUSNESS BEFORE RECORDING A PODCAST SHOW
- THE IMPORTANCE OF HASHTAGS FOR PODCASTING
- PODCAST EVENTS
- PODCAST DIRECTORY
- AND SO MUCH MORE!

CTR MEDIA NETWORK PODCASTERS
JOIN NOW

CONTENTS

Saundra Covington

Saundra is a wife of an Over The Road Driver, we have been married to the over 17 years. She has written a book entitled "The Truck Drivers Wife Holding Down the Home Front" that is a collection of shared experiences, challenges, and rewards that she have encountered being married in this Industry.

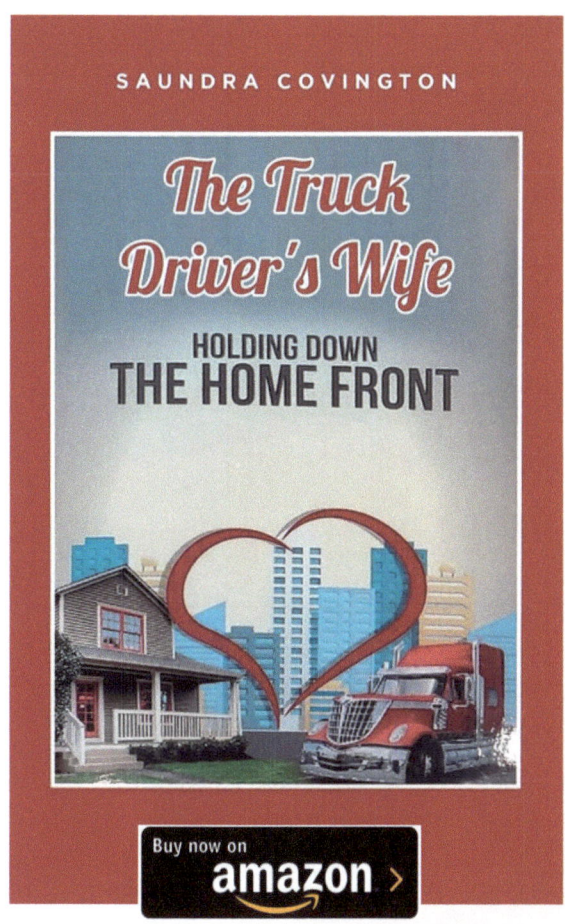

She help people who want to be more effective and productive to build their homes and support their partners working in the logistics industry. She created an education-based presentation/talk/webinar that sells our experience to our listeners and followers. Saundra wanted to share her experiences being the Wife of an Over Road Driver. Our world in this industry is not the norm, adjusting to unexpected occurrences, and staying together thru devastating losses. Working with us, we let drivers and their partners know what to expect from this side and provide our experience to help with how to deal with day-to-day situations while Drivers are safe out on the road.

Business Spotlight

BACK TO THE BASICS
TUTORING
WHERE WE MAKE LEARNING FUN
www.backtothebasicstutoring.org

Help your children excel at learning!

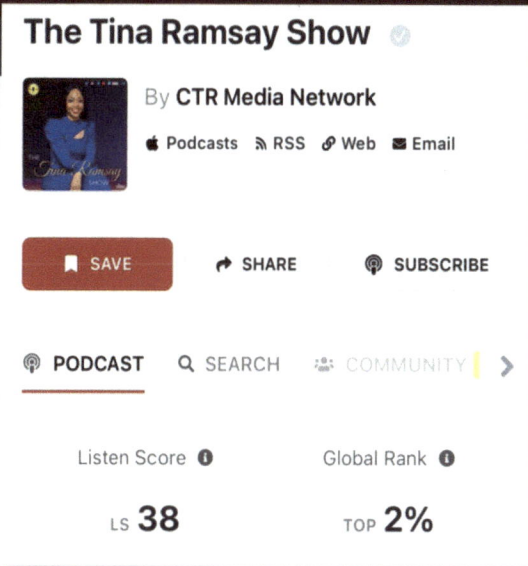
Proven Success: Achieving #1 new release and best-seller status on Amazon, "The Power of Podcasting" is trusted by countless enthusiasts like you. Join the ranks of successful podcasters with this acclaimed resource.

Expert Recommendation: Recognized by Book Authority among the top 11 podcast books of 2023, this book offers actionable insights and guidance from seasoned experts. You can gain the knowledge you need to excel in your podcasting journey.

Affordable Opportunity: Get a limited-time offer! Purchase "The Power of Podcasting" and unlock our #1 course for just $35. Combine book wisdom with practical learning for maximum podcasting potential.

Take this chance to elevate your podcasting game. **Grab "The Power of Podcasting"** on Amazon.

PODCAST REVOLUTION MAGAZINE

SCAN ME

CTR MEDIA NETWORK

PODCAST TRAINING, PRODUCTION, & DISTRIBUTION

WWW.CTRMEDIANETWORK.COM

CTR MEDIA NETWORK is the New Standard of Podcasting with 30+ podcasters. We reach 350 Million Global Listeners Worldwide in over 100 countries across all major podcasting and social media platforms that have featured over 1,000 Guests

Dr. Tina J. Ramsay, (h.c) 3X Best Selling International Author, Award Winning Host of The Tina Ramsay Show, and **CEO of CTR Media Network** with a powerful team of history makers that consists of COO, Curtis Ramsay an accomplished Photographer/Videographer, Sharae Moore, Head of Marketing & Public Relations, and our amazing hardworking staff. We Teach podcasters how to create, provide resources, monetize ideas, and connect their brand with the world. As a business owner or influencer, connect with podcasters to get your business out to reach Millions.

Nominated for Podcaster of the Year

THE
Tina Ramsay
SHOW

Westside Misfits Radio is an internet radio station powered by Live365 & licensed w/ BMI,ASCAP, SoundExchange

SCAN ME

MISFITS RADIO

SCAN ME

MISFITS RADIO

CTR MEDIA NETWORK

CTRMediaNetwork.com

CTR Media Network website offers Podcast Production, Training, & Distribution, media advertisement, Commercial Placement, Red Carpet Interviews, Business Spotlights, Affiliate Marketing, Event Planning, and more. Emerge and Leave a digital legacy that impacts the next generation by sharing your extraordinary story with the world.

What else do you offer?

CTR Media Network offers additional services and products such as Sponsorship Opportunities, Inspirational Notebooks, The Homeschooling Interactive Magazine, Homeschooling Consultations, Female Wellness Products, Voice Overs, Podcast Interviews, Podcast Coaching, Podcast Audits, Photography, Brand Development, Marketing, Content Creation, and Event Coordinating.

Do you have any training on starting your own podcast or other media spots? If so, what is it, and how can one be a part of it?

Yes, we have our: " Learn How to Start a Podcast and Monetize It, Class" designed for busy authors and entrepreneurs to launch a podcast from scratch quickly. CTR Media Network help authors, content creators, and entrepreneurs flip their books and business into podcasts, magazines, and WebTV Shows. If you are an author or business owner and want to start a podcast, you can visit our website to learn more. www.CTRMediaNetwork.com

Thank You

Photo Credit: Multifarious Studios
Stylist: Donna Young @Lovely People Boutique

CTR Media Network Sponsors

CTR MEDIA NETWORK

HONORARY LEGACY SPONSOR
TERRI COLEMAN

Terri Coleman's legacy continues to shine brightly, even after her passing. She was an exceptional individual, an author, and a successful businesswoman who made it her mission to promote homeownership and education in Atlanta and beyond. Her work left an indelible mark on countless individuals, and her example continues to inspire others to follow in her footsteps.

Those who had the privilege of working closely with Terri can attest to the profound impact she had on their lives. Dr. Tina J Ramsay, CEO of CTR Media Network, was one such individual. Terri was the first sponsor of CTR Media Network, and her support was instrumental in bringing the network's vision to life. Terri's willingness to collaborate and share her expertise with others was a testament to her kindness and generosity, and CTR Media Network will forever be grateful for her contributions.

Today, Terri's mission lives on through her platform, "Mindset to Millions," and her company, Global Key Capital LLC. Her passion for educating and empowering others about the secrets of wealth and finance was truly inspiring, and her legacy will continue to inspire others to pursue their dreams and achieve financial freedom.

Terri Coleman will always be remembered as a trailblazer, a mentor, and a friend to many. Her impact on the world will continue to be felt for generations to come, and her memory will forever be cherished. As an Honorary Legacy Sponsor of CTR Media Network, Terri's legacy will always have a special place in our hearts and of those who knew her.

GLOBAL KEY
C A P I T A L

'Mindset to Millions' accompanied with Global Key Capital LLC a winning strategy for a path to success and freedom.

Honorary Legacy Sponsor

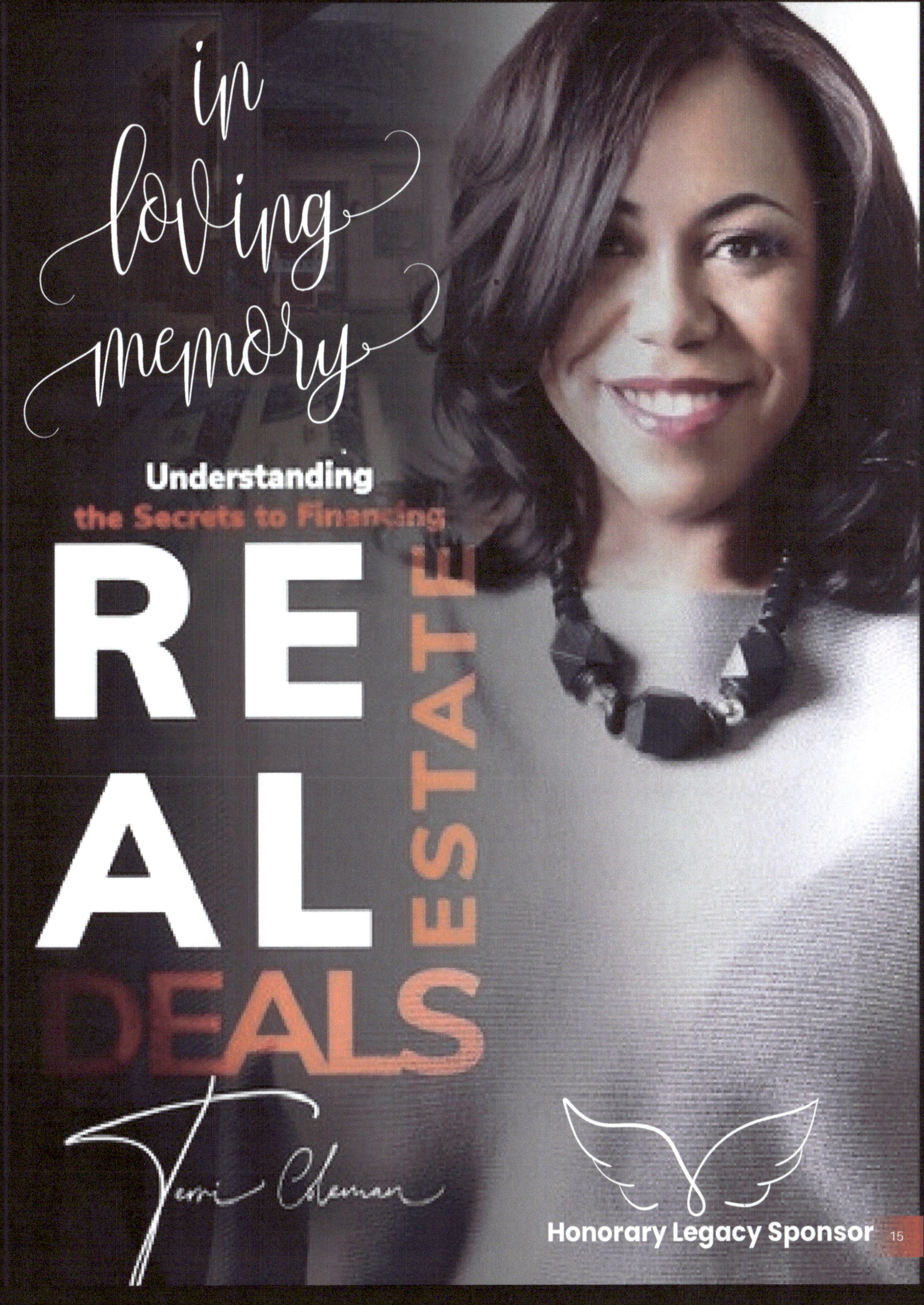

in loving memory
Understanding
the Secrets to Financing
REAL ESTATE DEALS
Terri Coleman
Honorary Legacy Sponsor

LEROY & ELNORA GRAY-MASON

Introducing Elnora Gray-Mason, a native of Hampton, Virginia, and the CEO of Happy and Healthy Global. With a 20-year marriage to a minister, Elnora is a proud mother of three daughters - Pamela, Gwendolyn, and Alisha. For the past 42 years, she has been a dedicated insurance agent, specializing in Medicare for the past 20.

In December 2004, she met Leroy Mason, a kind and respectful man with a gentle soul. Through working alongside him in network marketing.

Elnora saw first-hand his compassion and drive to make a difference. This experience inspired her to join forces with Aluva, a company that is changing lives and making a positive impact. With the support of our Lord and Savior Jesus, we strive to be the best versions of ourselves and make a difference in the world.

Elnora has always had a strong faith, accepting Jesus as her Lord and Savior at a young age. She has been an active member of her community, teaching Sunday school, Bible study, and serving as a praise dancer until she was 60 years young. Her dedication to her faith earned her the Worship and Arts Ministry Most Faithful award in 2007.

With a Bachelor of Science in Business Management from Hampton University, Elnora has received numerous accolades, including a certificate and ring for being an insurance earner over $100,000 and an Angel award for her assistance in counseling and mentoring single parents.

In her current role, Elnora assists seniors with lowering their out-of-pocket expenses for prescription drugs through different Medicare companies, as well as offering products to help pay for health deductibles, life insurance, cancer hospital indemnity, and assisting veterans in paying their Part B premiums. She also has a wealth of experience in managing and training agents, having been part of starting up two mortgage companies.

"With a passion for health and nutrition, Elnora has always had a dream of being part of God's healing ministry for 15 years"

WWW.HAPPYANDHEALTHY.GLOBAL

With a passion for health and nutrition, Elnora has always had a dream of being part of God's healing ministry, and 15 years ago, she started her second goal of finding a company to market healthy alternative products online, which birth her own wellness business called **HappyandHealthy.Global.** She plans to impact the world by providing educational information and essential natural wellness products to help you with your wealth and health. In her leisure time, she loves line dancing, playing spades, bid whist, and phase 10. She wants you to be Happy, Healthy, and Wealthy.

MEET KMUNT

Kmunt is an all-in-one app that lets you easily create and promote any type class in your local community. With the app, you can set up a class and choose a GPS location for it. Once the class is set up, the app will automatically send an alert to users within a 10-mile radius of the location. When a user joins your class, the app collects the trainer fee and pays it out to you.

This app is perfect for instructors and trainers who want to focus on teaching without worrying about marketing or collecting payments. With the Kmunt App, you can reach more people in your community and grow your business.

Download App in your Google Play or Apple Store today!
VISIT OUR WEBSITE
Kmunt.com

CTR MEDIA NETWORK

Our Mission

We promote access to justice for consumers across America. Our software allows consumers to leverage the Web to create convenient, affordable, and powerful demand letters that can be sent to a company to drive a favorable settlement.

Why choose us

- We're on your side
- We'll use our many years of experience to help you resolve your dispute. We've been there and done it successfully against the largest companies.
- We've got you covered in all 50 states
- Our software works no matter what state you hail from.
- One low flat fee per letter
- No subscriptions, surprises or hourly rates.
- No risk!
- We offer a 100% no questions asked money back guarantee valid up to 30 days from purchase. If your SettleShark demand letter doesn't lead to a settlement you get your full purchase price back.
- Big Savings
- Similar demand letter services cost hundreds of dollars.
- You're in control
- You can save and edit your letter and decide when to send it to the company.

www.Settleshark.com

SettleShark

Call now
1-888-704-0708

CTR MEDIA NETWORK
Silver Sponsor

MEET COACH JUDAH

WHAT THEY DO

BUSINESS COURSE ACADEMY

THE BALANCE DOCTOR

The Kim Jacobs Show, Kim will interview celebrity and everyday people to share their **BACKSTORY**! The topics will be **REAL. RELEVANT. RELATABLE!** The goal is to help you balance every aspect of your life from cradle to grave and even beyond!!!

We often see the beautiful lifestyle and the tremendous success a person has accomplished, but we don't always know what it took for them to get there! There are so many things to balance in life and sometimes the many responsibilities can be overwhelming! On The Kim Jacobs Show, the guest has overcome many obstacles to become the great success they are today! Some of the stories are heartbreaking, while others are very entertaining and lighthearted.

Every episode will leave you eagerly awaiting the next one! Guest will share how they balance everything they have on their plates and keep their sanity. Guest will reveal how they fought to make their dreams become a reality! What did they have to endure to become who they are today! The Kim Jacobs show will have makeovers , performances, and other fun segments to offer the audience. **The Kim Jacobs Show - Balance Doctor.** The Kim Jacobs Show is an online one hour Talk Show that airs **Monday - Friday at 11 AM EST**

PODCAST GUESTS

LES BROWN   **PAM MCCLOSKEY**   **EMMIT & PAT SMITH**

REMEMBERING GABE

Every two to three days in the U.S., a young athlete dies as the result of sudden cardiac arrest. In fact, sudden cardiac arrest is the number one cause of sudden death in exercising young athletes. In most cases, the arrest occurs with no warning. In the midst of play or practice, the athlete suddenly collapses. And if appropriate action is not taken within minutes, the athlete will die or be left with serious brain damage.

Gabe's Heart Foundation is carrying the torch for the young athletes, the parents who are unaware of the signs and necessary life saving steps, and for the community at large, because when the next young athlete experiences sudden cardiac arrest, it affects us all and bringing awareness to this cause could save a life. **- Donate at www.Gabesheartfoundation.org**

INTRODUCING

LEGAL WELLNESS W/ DR.LYDIE, PH.D, ESQ.

Here, we gather as a heart-driven worldwide business community to learn, connect, create an impact and succeed. You are your brand. There is much more to branding than marketing. The Law plays a powerful role in our branding.

Business owners often need to be aware of how powerful a role law, particularly Intellectual Property (IP) law, plays in our businesses.

The truth is that IP law gives you the power to monetize your original ideas in ways you never imagined, or if your IP needs to be adequately protected, the loss of income stream can destroy your brand and your business.

It truly is a fine line between success and failure. The truth is, what you do has value. From the moment you create it to your entire lifetime and beyond. How you do what you do is very valuable. It's measurable and impactful.

I advise executives and entrepreneurs just like you how to harness the Power and the Leverage of the Law to protect and commercialize the original ideas that you create.

NEW PODCAST

www.DrLydie.com

24

Leveling Up

The Podcast

...with Alethia

Alethia Tucker

International Keynoter | Reinvention Strategist | Bestselling Author
"I believe with all of my heart our struggles as women can become so much easier when we realize we are not alone." – Alethia Tucker

Voted one of the "Top 25 Most Inspiring Women" by Called 2 Inspire Magazine, Alethia Tucker is a highly sought-after international keynote speaker, reinvention strategist, and bestselling author. Regarded as one of the most influential voices of motivational speaking, Alethia impacts audiences worldwide with her message of encouragement and empowerment.

Alethia trains individuals and organizations to amplify their courage, confidence, and connection so they can make an influential impact on the world. She mentors passionately, guiding her clients to reach their highest potential. She facilitates robust workshop training to help them conquer obstacles, pursue passions, and live a life of purpose.

Leveraging over 20 years of human resources, training, and marketing experience, Alethia has a unique talent for making meaningful connections and a remarkable ability to help others maximize their strengths. She has a deep-rooted passion for people, leadership, and excellence, which qualifies her to help people take their dreams – and themselves – to unprecedented levels.

Alethia's extensive leadership expertise had earned her invitations to speak on major corporate stages across the country. She has delivered dynamic live and virtual keynote speeches for large audiences, including Shawn Fair's Leadership Experience Tour, Cheryl Wood's Women Crushing Mediocrity, and Radio Toni on the BBS TV Network in Australia, to name a few.

Alethia is a compelling thought leader who champions the success of women's personal and professional empowerment, providing opportunities to use their gifts, talents, and voice. In line with her unyielding passion for helping women succeed, Alethia founded Jolease Enterprises, which offers strategies for reinvention by overcoming self-limiting thoughts, doubt, and fear. She is also the host Leveling up the Podcast. The show focuses on topics that impact her community to include finance, health, faith, career and lifestyle. Alethia is the leading authority on igniting personal empowerment and creating environments that foster success.

She founded two community initiatives called The Journey Society and Journey Shares, women-based communities dedicated to supporting, strengthening, elevating, and helping one another to thrive As an influential figure, she serves as a visionary of an anthology and an Amazon #1 bestselling author of four books: 50 Things I've Learned on My Way to 50, Women Crushing Mediocrity, Speaking My Truth and Reinvented to Rise.

Recognized as a well-known fixture in her community, Alethia participates in several volunteer projects, including supporting the homeless, student scholarship fundraising, church youth groups, and Girls Speaks, a self-enrichment program for young ladies aged 11-24.

Alethia is a visionary who is often recognized for her leadership, commitment, and contributions to her community and the next generation. Her work has been featured on prominent media platforms such as ABC, CBS, NBC, FOX, and in leading magazines, newspapers, radio, podcasts, and news articles, including Yahoo Finance, Boston Herald, and New York Weekly, among others.

LEARN FROM THE BEST WITH COACH DERRICK

The 8 Figure Talks podcast, hosted by Derrick Harper provides insights and strategies for achieving success in business and life. Experts, entrepreneurs, and thought leaders share their experiences and offer valuable tips on a range of topics, from entrepreneurship and finance to personal development and mindset. Join the conversation and achieve your goals with 8 Figure Talks Unlocking the Secrets to Wealth!

Join the Inner Circle Today!

PODCAST REVOLUTION MAGAZINE

4 PODCAST MONETIZATION IDEAS

CTR MEDIA NETWORK

1. **Start a Patron Account**
2. **Ask for Donation**
3. **Charge for Commercial Ad**
4. **Product Placement**

JOIN OUR CLASS TODAY
CTRMEDIANETWORK.COM
PODCAST REVOLUTION MAGAZINE

CAMELIA WALL

A Call to Help Others

Featured THE *Tina Ramsay* SHOW

CAMELIA WALL Author, has faithfully worked with the mentally fragile for decades. Her highly sought-after wisdom and understanding of the intellectually disabled field have garnered praise and recognition.

She's dedicated to her Christian faith and unashamed of sharing her beliefs. She resides in Columbia, SC, with her husband, Ronald, and their two children, Jordan and Joshua.

"Camelia has a no-nonsense spirit, and it proves to be a protective agent for all those she serves.

This book surpasses being just a memoir of her experiences as a long-term care service provider. It's a clarion call to all to seek God for only His perfect will to be done in our lives."

— Dr. Shane Wall, Pastor, Bestselling Author, TV Show Host

SCAN ME

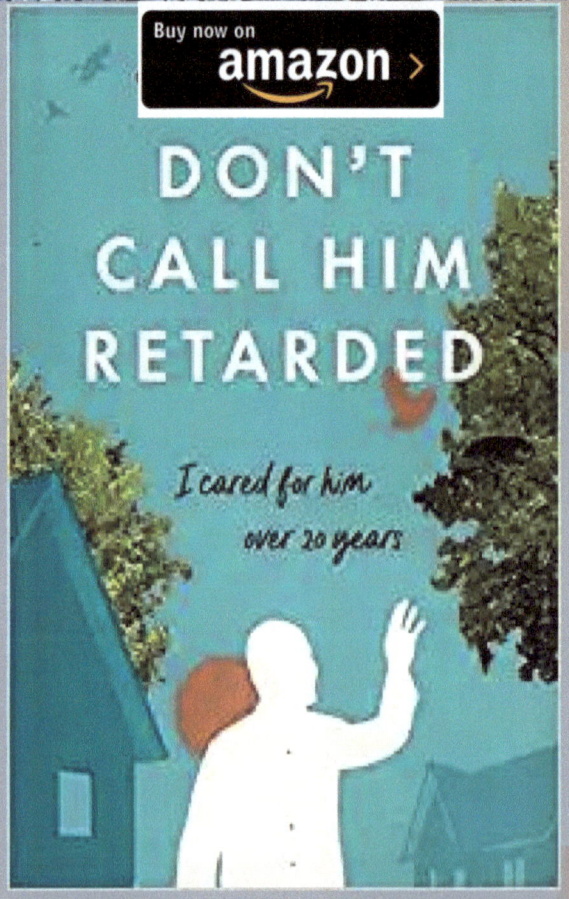

Buy now on amazon >

DON'T CALL HIM RETARDED

I cared for him over 20 years

HELLO WORLD

My name is Joy!

I own a growing business called Be The Difference Clothing. This company was established in August of 2013. Most if not all designs are created to inspire those who see and wear the designs. Some designs are inspired by personal experiences and others from situations seen or heard. I distinctly remember the moment I decided to print t-shirts. I was driving home from an event when for the first time in my life I saw a person "stuck". They were literally standing on the corner bent backwards just swaying a little. After I drove by it hit me ...

I remember thinking, "What am I doing, I am no different than the next person who just says to themselves wow so sad." I could no longer stomach being the passerby. It took guts and I battled fear of being rejected to create the Addiction Kills The Family design.

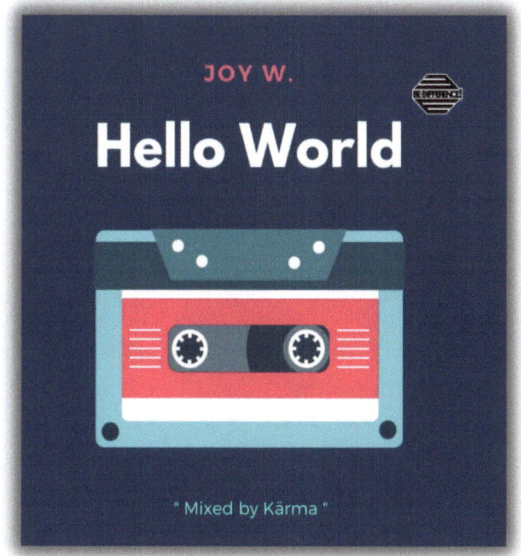

JOY W.

Hello World

" Mixed by Kärma "

I am at the point where my concern is in comfort and support. This company has many discussion pieces and light-hearted, playful themes that can appeal to any age, race, or understanding.

The company has expanded into speaking engagements and workshops. For booking, please get in touch with info@bethedifferencellc.cominfo@bethediff erencellc.com

THE MOTHERS PLACE

THE MOTHERS PLACE

The Mothers Place is a podcast show that encourages, strengthens, rebuilds, and realigns mothers. This podcast allows the voice of Mother to go forth as the Birther of the Nation. We have adapted to society and become a culture of allowing many things to become because of LOVE and being passive. Some aspects of ourselves have neglected the duty of being Mothers through taking care of everyone else, negating that self-care and self LOVE are first. Now that we obtain self-care through whatever aspects are needed for our mental, physical, and spiritual growth, we can assist everyone else.

PODCAST REVOLUTION MAGAZINE

Mother is also connected to **WOMAN, WIFE, MOTHER** and **DAUGHTER**. The Mothers Place embraces all that connects to Mother and seeks to enhance the rehabilitation of a NATION through the Mothers' eyes. Shana Asby is the host who invites guest speakers to encourage women and give advice through their own experiences and professions. This platform inspires MOTHERS to REALIGN with whom she was BUILT to BE, part putting God first, Family, Then Everything else.

Shana is a family life coach, receiving her certification through The J2P Institute. Shana empowers the family to learn about each member as an individual, understand the power of family, and embrace working together as a collective unit. She has written a curriculum titled, The Right to Knowledge, which has been shared within the foster care community, authored a children's book titled " Shay Shay Lorraines Bubblegum," and is a public speaker and community organizer. Shana also enjoys spending time with children where she inspires them to become their best selves, using great mannerisms when building self-character skills.

SHANA ASBY
FAMILY LIFE COACH & HOST

**Shana believes that Mothers
Birth the Nation, and that they
have the POWER to RESHAPE one.**

We educate, advise, and train Nonprofit Professionals on how to make their nonprofits PROFITABLE.

Our goal on The Keisha Parris Show is to motivate people to take steps to become the best versions of themselves.

We educate you on things in business, life, and childcare and give motivational tips

Jimmie Cameron

In June of 1964 by the suggestion from her oldest son Jasper, Emma Bell Cameron Simmons sold her house and property located at the foot of Orcard Knob Memorial Park, rented a u-haul and drove to Los Angeles where her children would have better opportunities for advancement. Jimmie, age 14 at the time, immediately pursued a career in music and theatrics. Befriended by Nichelle Nicoles of Star Trek fame she introduced him to Frank Silvera, founder of the American Theater of Being which was a primarily black theater group in Hollywood at the Coronet Theater. There, Jimmie became one of the up-and-coming in theatrics, TV, and movies in the midst of others such as Maya Angelou, Bea Richards, Isabel Sanford, Dick Anthony Williams,

Whitman Mayo, Marla Gibbs, Billy Dee Williams and so on; all members of the theater group at the Coronet theater. Jimmie, being the youngest in the group, landed the role of David in the James Baldwin play "the Amen Corner". Baldwin befriended Jimmie and actually wrote the liner notes for Heartbeat, Jimmie and Vella's first album, produced by Bobby Womack. The duo were casted in the Alcapulco production of the controversial musical "Hair" in 1967.

They got very little airplay on their recordings but the public loved their music, by which they became an underground sensation. They were recognized throughout the industry and those in the public who were able to experience them, loved them. Being out of the box musically, unique and innovative for young black artists, no one knew what to do with them but they persevered. They appeared in the Jimi Hendrix movie "Rainbow Bridge". The director and writer of the movie sent the song that they performed (Old Men) to Jimi Hendrix's manager, Michael Jeffries, who immediately wanted to sign them and move them to New York, which he did.

There, they became, again, an underground sensation. Jeffries acquired a deal at Atlantic Record for the duo; the album was called Jimmie and Vella, which again, had no promotion.

BE FAIR TO ME

Song Painters, by Jimmie and Vella Cameron, is the product of the lifelong association of two talented artists. A brother-sister act that has been evolving for sixteen years, Jimmie and Vella have shared both the writing and production chores for their debut release on Unlimited Gold Records. Barry White is the executive producer of the album.

Jimmie and Vella Cameron began their recording careers in 1964 when they migrated to Los Angeles from their native home of Chattanooga, Tennessee. Two albums and several years later their paths crossed with the "Maestro", Barry White. Barry, realizing their talent and potential, offered them a contract with Unlimited Gold Records.

Jimmie and Vella Cameron

Song Painters represents a diverse musical presentation from Jimmie and Vella. Their musical interests run the gamut from R&B, to classical, and even country. As the title of the album implies, the Camerons are presenting on **Song Painters** a collection of versatile tunes that are introspective and romantic.

Unlimited Gold Records takes pleasure in announcing **Song Painters**, colorful music by Jimmie and Vella Cameron.

JZ/JZT 36132

JIMMIE AND VELLA ALBUMS:

Jimmie Cameron

Yet they persevered and maintained popularity in performance throughout the East coast and Europe opening for acts such as Cat Stevens, Patti LaBelle, Alice Coltrane (John Coltrane's wife), Hugh Masekela, Dave Mason, Bill Withers, and Dick Gregory. Michael Jeffries declared that after he saw Jimmie and Vella to success he would then retire. But he was killed in a plane crash over Spain in 1973. The duo moved back to Los Angeles and persevered for years without a recording deal although several were offered to them. They finally signed with Unlimited Gold Records, Barry White's label through Columbia, in 1979. The duo recorded their third album "Song Painters" where White produced four songs on the album and Jimmie and Vella produced the rest. There again, the duo's album was not promoted commercially by Columbia or Barry White. Jimmie and Vella remained exceptional with a lot of respect from the industry and the public. The duo continued to enjoy a worldwide fanbase.

Heartbeat - 1968
Jimmie and Vella - 1972
Song Painters - 1981
Song Credits:
Barry White - "It's Only Love Doing Its Thing"
Cher and Greg Almond - "Move Me"
50 Cent - "21 Questions"
Herb Alpert - "Bullish"
Staple Singers - "Chickaboom"
Dilated Peoples - "This Way"
Capone and Noreaga - "Invincible"
Love Unlimited Orchestra - "Wind"
Gene Page Orchestra- "Viva Fernando"
The OJs "Do You Really Know How I Feel"

Jimmie Carmon &
Nichelle Nicoles of Star Trek

**Coming Soon:
The Jimmie and Vella Story**

DR. YULANDA KING

Hope Psychiatric Consultants

VIRTUAL APPOINTMENTS | **THERAPY** | **MEDICATION** | **MEDICATION + THERAPY**

"HANDING OUT POSITIVE ENERGY"

SCAN ME

"Normalization of seeking Professional help for Mental Health"

From a registered nurse serving on transplant, PCU, and ICU units to a Nurse Practitioner who is a board-certified Psychiatric Mental Health Nurse (PMHNP-BC), I have done various roles that have contributed to my extensive expertise in the field of mental medicine! In addition to my specialist title as a mental health nurse, I hold titles of Doctor of Nursing Practice (DNP), Certified Registered Nurse Practitioner (CRNP), and Adult-Gerontology Acute Care Nurse Practitioner- Board Certified (AGACNP-BC). It is my pleasure to serve all patients ranging from four to one hundred years old with mental disorders such as, but not limited to, Generalized Anxiety Disorder, Bipolar Disorder, Post-Traumatic Stress Disorder (PTSD), and all forms of Addiction.

TELEHEALTH

HOPE
PSYCHIATRIC CONSULTANTS

39

Sandy Sanders Founder and Host of Coffee Conversations With Sandy and Friends, A collective conversation aim to empower, encourage and inspire each other. It is also a place of accountability so that we can be the person who were born to become. Coming from behind the mask and walking in our authenticity,

Sandy is known for style of interviewing and moderating a conversation on her weekly broadcast Book Talks With Sandy™ that is viewed globally on various social media platforms.

Book Talks with Sandy

She is the "coffee conversations and book talks lady" for book releases, author tours, virtual and hybrid summit events. She will tell you that her beginnings all started because her first book was published and she didn't know how to launch it so it was her Facebook Lives and sharing inspirations that birthed out the show because someone viewed it asked to showcase their authors.

Owning her personal story of overcoming a traumatic childhood, low self-esteem, alcoholism and domestic violence, has given Sandy a great sense of relation with communal advocacy.

BOOK TALKS

Sandy serves as an active Board member of non-profit organization providing female inmates recently released. Business Empowered Mississippi Chamber of Commerce Board member.

Sandy has served as Brand Ambassador with Success Women's Conference 2020, Chief Ambassador Best of Mississippi Awards 2020, magazine futures include Gulf Coast Women's Magazine Domestic Violence Special Edition Oct 2021, SwagHer Magazine August 2021.

When Sandy Sanders is not out changing the world through a simple conversation and hosting her weekly authors showcase interviews, Sandy is a loving wife, devoted mother of 3 Adult children, and a grandmother of 4. Sandy is a Licensed Evangelist and serves in various capacities in her local church.

SCAN ME

HUSH No More Champions is a platform to allow Survivors, Advocates, and Nonprofit Organizations to have a safe space to discuss their experience with the HUSH Topics and how they recovered from their trauma.

 **It is your RIGHT to tell, Break the Silence!**

HUSH Topics includes sexual assault, child sexual abuse, incest, domestic violence, sex trafficking, sexual harassment, and addiction. Dr. Vanessa Dunn Guyton interviews amazing guests that will help you address your own personal journey and provide valuable resources. **Awareness + Knowledge=Prevention.**

Dr. Vanessa Dunn Guyton

Hush No More was created to support and provide Survivors a safe place to HUSH No More and to provide training on The HUSH Topics. We focus on those topics communities have a hard time discussing. We are a place of healing.

Hush No More is Non-Profit 5013C Organization in South Carolina
They are currently accepting donations.
www.hushnomore.org

WAYS TO STAY MOTIVATED

Set clear and specific goals: Having a clear and specific goal in mind can help you stay focused and motivated. Break down your larger goals into smaller, more achievable ones and create a plan of action. Visualize your success: Visualizing your success can be a powerful motivator.

Imagine yourself achieving your goals, and how it will feel once you've accomplished what you set out to do. Find your "why": Knowing why you want to achieve your goals can help you stay motivated. Think about the reasons behind your goals and how they will improve your life. Surround yourself with positive influences: Surrounding yourself with positive people who encourage and support you can help keep you motivated. Join a group or community of like-minded individuals who are working towards similar goals.

Reward yourself: Give yourself small rewards along the way as you make progress towards your goals. Celebrating your accomplishments can help keep you motivated and give you the energy to keep going.

Stay organized: Being organized and having a clear plan of action can help you stay motivated. Use a planner or calendar to keep track of your progress and make adjustments as needed. Take breaks: It's important to take breaks and recharge your batteries.

Schedule in time for relaxation and self-care to avoid burnout. Remember, it's okay to have off days. Don't beat yourself up if you're feeling unmotivated, instead, try some of these strategies to get back on track.

The Wellness Driven Life Show is the number one place giving real-time and relevant tools to help anyone achieve total wellness. In detail, The Wellness Driven Life Show includes powerful insights and resources within the emotional, spiritual, intellectual, physical, environmental, financial, occupational, and social areas of our lives. Furthermore, as everyone is unique, we offer compassion aligned with each participant's personality, preferences, and ideas, and there's no judgment. Unlike other places, I'm always authentic, true to my words, and will provide you with inspiring stories.

8 Podcast Production Tips

Podcast production is a thrilling journey that allows you to bring your creative vision to life and share it with the world! Here are the steps to turn your ideas into an exciting podcast:

1. **Conceptualization**: Start by developing a clear idea of what your podcast will be about, who your target audience is, and what makes your show unique.

2. **Equipment**: Invest in good quality equipment, including a microphone, headphones, and recording software.

3. **Script Writing:** Create a script that outlines the structure of your podcast and includes all of the critical points you want to cover.

4. **Recording**: Record your podcast in a quiet environment, focusing on speaking clearly and with enthusiasm.

5. **Editing**: Use editing software to clean up any mistakes and make sure your podcast sounds polished and professional.

6. **Music & Sound Effects:** Add music and sound effects to enhance the overall listening experience and keep your audience engaged.

7. **Promotion:** Join CTR Media Network to promote your podcast through social media, email, and other marketing channels.

8. **Analyze & Improve**: Track your listenership and get feedback to improve your podcast and keep your audience engaged continually.

With these steps, you can bring your podcast dreams to life and create a show that's both exciting and impactful!

They also help readers jump to the topics of interest

When you've decided on your cover story, come up with a list of topics for your feature articles. This can range from interviews, product reviews, human interest pieces, and even lists. Think about what your audience would be interested in and get writing! Again, choose engaging photos and graphics to accompany your words, as these also help catch your audience's eye.

CTR MEDIA NETWORK
presents:

Dr. Tina J Ramsay

THE TINA RAMSAY SHOW

www.ctrmedianetwork.com/thetinaramsayshow

Trending

Dr. Tina J. Ramsay (HC) is a highly accomplished and influential motivational speaker, 3x best-selling author, wife, mother, and media personality with over 25 years of experience in education and ten years in the media industry. She is the CEO of **CTRMediaNetwork.com**, founder of The Homeschooling Interactive Magazine, and host of **The Tina Ramsay Show**. In both areas, Dr. Tina focuses on impacting the lives of the people she coaches and meet. She has direct access to over **300,000 podcasters and educators worldwide in leadership positions.**

As a podcasting media and educational industry leader, Dr. Ramsay uses her platforms to empower individuals to share positive, impactful stories and resources globally. She has helped podcasters and entrepreneurs utilize **the power of podcasting** to build their brand awareness, share knowledge, and market their businesses effectively. She is a sought-after speaker and coach teaching **podcasting and homeschooling** with her signature 24-step visibility process along with her #1 Best Selling book The Power of Podcasting.

47

PODCAST REVOLUTION MAGAZINE

Meet The Ramsay's

Curtis & Dr. Tina J Ramsay, The Powerhouse Couple, creating a new standard of podcasting and media.

Dr. Tina's determination and zeal for life come from her inborn will to fight for others. After **her near-death experiences** and various hardships in her life over the years and after having a stroke at 25 years old that left her partially paralyzed with amnesia. **She operates and moves on purpose,** especially when God Blessed her to be able to walk and regain most of her memory again. So, she uses her life as a testimony to inspire you to dream big again and never give up.

In addition to her media work, Dr. Ramsay serves as a media relations specialist, homeschooling consultant, and podcast producer. She has a reputation for her honesty, transparent engagement, and down-home Southern charm, and is highly valued for her opinions on life, products, and services. Her company, **CTR Media Network**, offers a full suite of podcast production, training, distribution, and media coverage services and reaches **350 million households worldwide** across major podcasting and social media platforms.

Dr. Ramsay has received numerous awards, nominations, certifications, and recognitions for her work, being named one of the top 100 global speakers by Dr. Cheryl Wood. recently **The Tina Ramsay Show has ranked in the top 2% most popular podcast shows in the world**. She is affectionately known as "Coach T" for her professional work ethic, media presence, infectious laughter, Southern accent, and heart to help others succeed.

The Tina Ramsay Show, is all about motivating you, sharing knowledge, and having upbuilding conversations centered around Business, Education, Wellness, and Life. We introduce you to stand-out Entrepreneurs, Celebrities, and Business Leaders that are making a positive impact in the world! We will love to feature you!

Sponsorship Opportunities are available
email: thetinaramsayshow1@gmail.com to learn more

SELF CARE

Practice mindfulness: Mindfulness is a great way to reduce stress and increase self-awareness. You can practice mindfulness by focusing on your breathing and the present moment. You can also try meditation sitting in a quiet place.

Get enough sleep: Sleep is crucial for physical and mental health. Ensure you get enough sleep each night (usually 7-9 hours) and create a sleep-conducive environment, such as keeping your bedroom cool, dark, and quiet.

Exercise regularly: Regular physical activity is essential for maintaining physical and mental well-being. Aim to get at least 30 minutes of moderate exercise daily, such as walking, running, or practicing a sport. Regular exercise can help boost your mood, increase energy levels, and reduce stress.

Disconnecting from Social Media and connecting by spending time with friends and family, or participating in social activities, can help improve your mental health and well-being.

Studies have shown that strong social connections can help reduce stress, boost your mood, and improve your overall happiness and fulfillment.

Take breaks and engage in hobbies: Regular intervals throughout the day to do something you enjoy, such as reading a book, painting, or playing a musical instrument, can help reduce stress and improve your mental well-being. Having hobbies and interests outside work can also help you feel fulfilled and satisfied.

Doctor Fashion
Creator Lyfe CEO

Neal Hamilton
Artist & Photography

Natalie Peri
Actress

Aysha Williams
Celebrity MUA

The Tina Ramsay Show Guests

Rita Graham
Ray Charles Protégé

Varonica Mitchell
The VVShow

Testimonials

*Love, Love, Love Tina! She is all about connecting and elevating people. Her platform showcases up-and -coming entrepreneurs as well as well-seasoned vets. I saw immediate results after appearing on her show~ **Tiffany D. Bell***

Tina embraces her guests and is genuinely interested in their platforms and products. My experience as a guest was amazing!!
*~**Constance Woulard***

Dr. Tina's platform have opened me up to so many different opportunities. I have gotten speaking engagements, introductions to some influential people. My appearance on the Tina Ramsay show was a wonderful experience, and I can't wait to work with Tina again.
*~**Adrienne Brown***

Melba Moore
Tony Award Winning Actress

SCAN ME

Mac Wells, Actor

Nahaia Russ DipNat,
Herbs, PT

Dr. Monika Juszczyk

Maya McClean
Actress & Singer

Dr. Patrick Dicks D.Sc
King of Automation

Dr. Dorothy Cook
The Millionaire Maker

Testimonials

Way to go!
Such an amazing tool for entrepreneurs~AngieGriffen

So much to learn!
Keep the show going, great content. ~KT

Had an awesome time. Great show!
~~Shawana McKinstry

An outstanding interview with Tina, full of enthusiasm and warm energy. She asks pertinent questions to effectively make it easy to converse and get your message across. I'm very pleased that I reached out to Tina and all her magazines and podcasts make it a triple wammy!
Thank you Tina. ~
Nahaia Russ DipNat, Herbs, PT

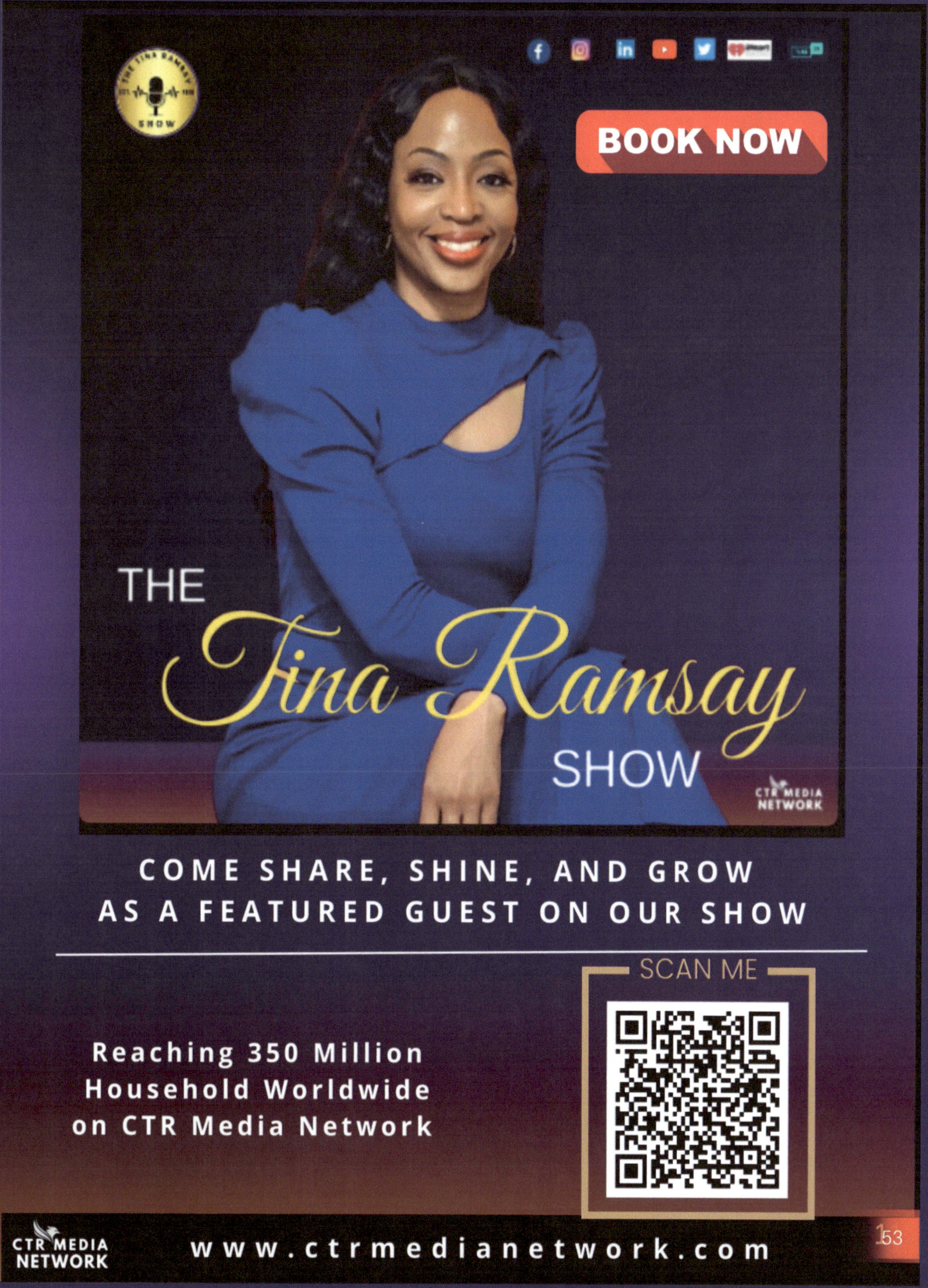
THE
Tina Ramsay
SHOW
BOOK NOW
THE TINA RAMSAY SHOW
CTR MEDIA NETWORK
COME SHARE, SHINE, AND GROW
AS A FEATURED GUEST ON OUR SHOW
SCAN ME
Reaching 350 Million
Household Worldwide
on CTR Media Network
CTR MEDIA NETWORK
www.ctrmedianetwork.com

4 STEPS TO BUILDING A BUSINESS WITH YOUR PODCAST

There is no doubt that Podcast's popularity keeps on growing since its inception in 2005. Accordingly, there are over over 48 million total episodes.; over 424 Million homes are podcast listeners, while smartphones are the most common devices used for watching, listening, or downloading a podcast stated statista.com. Given these numbers, many business owners, entrepreneurs, and marketers have been interested in capitalizing on this form of media. By utilizing podcasts, you can leverage your competitive position in the market, providing you with authority in a specific topic or field of interest. Also, Podcasts are a cheaper way to promote and market your products or services. It strengthens your credibility to your target audience and enables you to grow your network by collaborating with other experts in the field.

by

Dr. tina J. Ramsay

So, you may be wondering how you can monetize from your Podcast? How can you utilize it to grow your business?

Here are 4 steps in building a business with a podcast:

#1 Podcast Specialist

1.

START WITH A GOAL

This may sound basic, but it's essential. You can't start anything without a clear goal or vision. Ask yourself, what is it you're looking for to grow your business? Knowing what you want and why enables you to understand what you want to accomplish; therefore, it helps you come up with concrete decisions regarding what your podcast show would look like.

2.

IDENTIFY YOUR TARGET AUDIENCE

Treat your Podcast as a business. Identify your target audience and try to make it as specific as possible. Create an audience persona as you like; that would help you have a clear picture of your ideal client or listener. Visualize what your ideal audience looks like. What is their age? What is their income level? What are their interests? How familiar are they with your brand? Using segmentation to identify your ideal audience will help you develop a clear concept about the content of your show.

3.

LAUNCH AND PROMOTE

First, plan your Podcast by getting a domain name and creating a clear theme or format for your show. Then outline the content and start preparing your script. The next step is to identify music (royalty-free) that you want to use for the intro and outro, including other essential brand collateral such as cover art, logo, a backdrop for your show, etc. When everything is ready at your end, it's time to launch and promote your Podcast. Combine podcasting with other old-school marketing strategies such as downloadable pdfs for your audience. This way, you can enable them to subscribe to your email list and other social media platforms. Also, you can use discount codes that are uniquely available for your listener to track the effectiveness of your product or service advertisement. It not only navigates traffic to your website but also creates a funnel for your future marketing campaigns.

4.

CONDUCT INTERVIEWS

One way to establish your podcast credibility is to interview guests on your show. However, keep in mind that your interview should be full of value and not fluff. If your 30-minute show looks like a commercial promoting someone, that will affect how your audience perceives you as a podcaster. As much as possible, try to make a list of potential guests for an interview, assess their expertise in a particular field, and create a meaningful and focused flow of interview with them. Produce a quality episode that your guest can also share on their media platforms; thus, it's a win-win situation.

Accountability On Demand (AOD) Podcast

LaShana West is a Business Therapist and Mindset Coach that has been serving in the mental health field for over 20 years. She spent the early years of her career working directly with individuals with developmental disabilities. This is where she learned the importance of having true compassion and engaging in servant leadership. She then went on to gain a wealth of experience with program restructuring, training, staff development, quality assurance, and mastering an evidence-based behavior modification teaching model for children and families. All of these learning opportunities have positioned her to serve and step into a new direction by helping others in the creative and entrepreneurial field. With the mental health background coupled with the business acumen LaShana is able to help the "whole person".

ACCOUNTABILITY ON DEMAND PODCAST

LaShana uses a Life Coaching and Business Blend in her approach to help her clients get laser focused results! She helps them pinpoint and breakthrough the mental blocks that are holding them back. LaShana believes that past unresolved trauma and imposter syndrome are common barriers for most people no matter if you're a 9-5er or an entrepreneur. But with support and accountability you can do ANYTHING that your heart desire. Book a complimentary clarity call with LaShana to explore how she can support you through your breakthrough and beyond!

The Accountability On Demand (AOD) is hosted by Business Therapist and Mindset Coach LaShana West. The AOD Podcast is designed for creatives and entrepreneurs who are looking to take their business and personal growth to the next level. Our guests are experts in their respective fields and this podcast provides practical advice, tools, and strategies that listeners can use to achieve their goals and build successful businesses.

Each episode of Accountability On Demand features engaging interviews with successful creatives and entrepreneurs, who share their personal stories, insights, and actionable tips on topics such as productivity, mindset, marketing, and leadership. The show also features solo episodes, where LaShana West dives deeper into specific topics and provide step-by-step guidance and strategies that listeners can implement in their own businesses and lives.

Whether you're a freelancer, small business owner, or aspiring entrepreneur, the Accountability On Demand podcast will help you stay accountable to your goals, overcome challenges, and grow both personally and professionally. So, if you're ready to take action and achieve success on your own terms, this podcast is for you.

We serve Creatives, Entrepreneurs, CEO's and Leaders who are ready to get out of their own way so they can build the life and business of their dreams.

Time to Overcome

What are some practical ways to overcome nervousness before recording a podcast show?

It's natural to feel nervous before your podcast show, especially if you're just starting out or have a guest that you admire. Here are some tips to help you calm your nerves:

Prepare and practice: The more prepared you are, the less nervous you will feel. Take the time to prepare your content, research your guest, and practice your delivery. This will help you feel more confident and comfortable when you start recording.

Take deep breaths: Deep breathing is an effective way to calm your nerves. Take a few deep breaths before you start recording to slow your heart rate and ease your anxiety.

Visualize success: Visualize yourself delivering a successful podcast show, engaging your audience, and achieving your goals. This will help you feel more confident and positive about the experience.

By: Dr. Tina J. Ramsay

Focus on your audience: Remember that your podcast is for your audience. Focus on delivering valuable content to them and meeting their needs. This will help you shift your focus away from your nerves and onto the value you can provide.

Use positive self-talk: Use positive self-talk to encourage and motivate yourself. Tell yourself that you can do this and that you will do your best. This will help you feel more confident and less nervous.

The Speak Eazy discusses a variety of self-help self-improvement issues and topics. It is a space where individuals can freely discuss their ideas and thoughts.

"CIRCUMSTANCES AND SITUATIONS DO NOT DETERMINE YOUR SELF WORTH; YOU DO"
~B.PETTY~

Britteny is a published author of Stop The Drama Stop Comparing and Focus On You. Britteny wrote her first book sparked from the dire need personally seen in the educational system. Britteny takes pride in her ability to connect with individuals from all walks of life regardless of their past as a mental health therapist. Britteny has passion based on her own life experiences to dig deep in discovery of self-worth and heal from mental and physical abuse. Life's challenges have paved the way for Britteny to help individuals heal from abuse so they can find joy, live purposefully, and achieve their goals. Britteny loves focusing on promoting positivity to serve negativity a daily reminder it serves no purpose in your life. Britteny's smile radiates joys of life and spreads love to help others navigate life's toughest challenges. As a mental health therapist Britteny shares knowledge and upholds the calling to help individuals walk into the best versions of themselves daily through her podcast.

Mastering the Art of Entry: Conquering Manual, Revolving, and Automatic Doors

Imagine you are standing in front of a building with three entrances. Each entrance has a different type of door: a manual door, a revolving door, and an automatic door.

Let's take a closer look at each door and what it represents.

The manual door is straightforward and simple. You have to use your own strength and effort to open it. It requires physical exertion and can be a bit challenging, especially if you are carrying something heavy or have limited mobility. However, the manual door also gives you a sense of control and agency. You are the one opening the door, and you have the power to decide when and how to enter.

The revolving door, on the other hand, is more complex and dynamic. It requires you to step in and move with the door as it rotates around a central point. The revolving door can be a bit disorienting at first, but once you get the hang of it, it can be a fun and efficient way to enter a building. The revolving door also represents a kind of collaboration between you and the door. You have to work with the door to move forward, but in doing so, you also benefit from the door's momentum and energy.

Finally, the automatic door is the most convenient and effortless of the three. It opens automatically when you approach it, using sensors or other technology to detect your presence. The automatic door requires no physical effort or coordination on your part. It's quick, easy, and efficient. However, the automatic door also represents a kind of passive acceptance. You are not actively engaging with the door, but rather, the door is accommodating you.

So, which door would you choose?

Each door has advantages and disadvantages, representing a different approach to entering a building. The manual door requires effort and agency, the revolving door requires collaboration and momentum, and the automatic door requires passivity and accommodation.

In life, we often encounter different types of "doors" that we have to navigate. We may face obstacles that require us to exert effort and agency, or we may encounter opportunities that require us to collaborate and move with momentum. At other times, we may simply have to accept what comes our way, with little control or agency.

The key is to be aware of these different types of "doors" and to adapt our approach accordingly. Sometimes we need to push through the manual door with our own strength and determination. Other times we need to move with the flow of the revolving door and collaborate with others. And sometimes we need to accept the automatic door and trust that it will take us where we need to go. So, the next time you encounter a door, whether it's manual, revolving, or automatic, take a moment to reflect on what it represents and how you can best navigate it. And remember, sometimes the best approach is a combination of all three. In other words, this is your season to WIN!. Walk through the door.

KING CAN READ

www.KingCanRead.com

PODCAST

MEET THE AUTHOR

KING CHAMBERS

PRESIDENT

King Chambers is a remarkable little boy who has already accomplished so much in his short life. At the tender age of 2, he began reading and hasn't looked back since. Now 4 years old, King has become an advocate for children's literacy, math and education. He encourages his peers to read and learn new things, always striving to be a positive role model for those around him. Through his passion for reading and learning, King hopes to make a positive impact on the world and empower children everywhere.

KING CAN READ, PRESIDENT

www.KingCanRead.com

King Can Read is hosted by a 4-year-old boy the youngest podcaster on CTR Media Network! Join King as he encourages boys everywhere to discover the magic of reading and learning. With his captivating storytelling and infectious enthusiasm, King will ignite a passion for books that will last a lifetime. Like, Share, and Subscribe to the "King Can Read" podcast and get ready to join King on an exciting adventure of discovery and education. Don't miss a single episode, because King is on a mission to inspire a love of reading in children everywhere!

SCAN ME

SECRET LEGAL CODES REVEALED

Secret Legal Codes Revealed TV & Podcast is for the heart-driven business community to learn, connect, impact and succeed.
You are your brand!

The law plays a powerful role in your branding. Business owners are often unaware of how powerful a role law, particularly **Intellectual Property (IP) law**, plays in your business.

The truth is that IP law gives you the power to monetize your original ideas in ways you never imagined, or if your IP is not adequately protected, the loss of income stream can destroy your brand and your business.
Let's Discuss It!

MASTERING THE ART OF BOOKING GUESTS WITH PR

BY: CURTIS RAMSAY

When approaching a PR (public relations) representative about booking guests for your podcast, it's important to keep in mind that they are likely to receive many requests on behalf of their clients. Here are some tips for making a successful pitch:

A Public Relations (PR) Specialist is crucial in booking high-caliber guests and celebrities for podcast interviews, events, or projects.

Personalize your message: Show that you have done your research on the PR representative and their clients. Mention specific guests that you are interested in having on your podcast and explain why you think they would be a good fit.

Highlight the benefits: Explain how being a guest on your podcast can benefit their client. Will it give them exposure to a new audience? Help them promote a new project? Be sure to emphasize the unique value proposition of your podcast.

Be professional: Use a clear and concise message, and make sure to include all relevant information, such as the date and time of the recording, the expected length of the interview, and any technical requirements.

Follow up: PR representatives are busy, and it's possible that they may not respond to your initial message. If you don't hear back within a few days, send a polite follow-up message to check in and reiterate your interest.

Be flexible: Keep in mind that PR representatives may have specific requirements or limitations for their clients. Be open to working with them to find a mutually beneficial solutio

Remember, the goal is to establish a relationship with the PR representative that can benefit both you and their clients. With a thoughtful and professional approach, you can increase your chances of booking great guests for your podcast.

THE MICHAEL FINKLEY SHOW

EDUCATE INFORM & INSPIRE

MICHAEL D. FINKLEY, A NATIVE OF MULLINS, SC, IS AN ALUMNUS OF ALLEN UNIVERSITY WHERE HE GRADUATED WITH HIS BACHELOR OF ARTS IN ENGLISH. FINKLEY LATER GRADUATED FROM SOUTHERN NEW HAMPSHIRE UNIVERSITY WITH HIS GRADUATE DEGREES, MASTER OF EDUCATION & MASTER OF SCIENCE IN HIGHER EDUCATION ADMINISTRATION.

FINKLEY WAS FIRST INTRODUCED TO THE WORLD OF COMMUNICATIONS VIA HIS MOTHER AS SHE WAS A DISC JOCKEY FOR JOY 1280 WJAY IN MARION, SC.

FINKLEY LATER INTERNED WITH GLORY COMMUNICATIONS, WFMV 96.1 FM, IN COLLEGE. WHILE THERE, HE ASSISTED WITH THE RADIO SHOW, THE ARMSTRONG WILLIAMS SHOW. FINKLEY ALSO HOSTED THE RADIO TALK SERIES, I LOVE MULLINS, JOY 1280 WJAY, MARION, SC.

THE MICHAEL FINKLEY SHOW IS HERE TO EDUCATE, INFORM, AND INSPIRE!

CELEBRITY GUESTS

COMEDIAN
LAVELL CRAWFORD

ACTRESS
BERN NADETTE STANIS

ACTOR
DARRIN DEWITT HENSON

ACTRESS
DENISE BOUTTE'

ACTOR
JOHN MARSHALL JONES

R & B SINGER SHAI
DR. GARFIELD BRIGHT

MICHAEL D. FINKLEY

speaker | author | educator | celebrity host

THE FINKLEY EXPERIENCE

The Finkley Experience is an educational consulting firm that trains students and administrators on the needs of first generation students wanting to attend college. We're here to assist with one's personal development via two approaches; one-on-one or whole group consulting.

We focus on two clusters:
College Readiness and Professional Training.

What makes us different?
Finkley is equipped with a unique array of experiences at colleges and universities—in the Northeast to the Deep South—in a variety of roles including college admissions, career services, and teaching.

No one can deliver, train and capture an audience like The Finkley Experience.

🐦 **@THE_FINKLEYEX**
📷 f ▶ **@THEFINKLEYEXPERIENCE**
WWW.THEFINKLEYEXPERIENCE.COM

THE MICHAEL FINKLEY SHOW

The Michael Finkley Show is here to **EDUCATE, INFORM,** and **INSPIRE**. We will cover topics concerning education to interviews of everyday heroes with incredible stories. We air every Monday and Friday on You42, RokuTV, and YouTube. Please subscribe to our YouTube Channel at the Michael Finkley Show!

📷 f **MICHAELFINKLEYSHOW**
WWW.MICHAELFINKLEYSHOW.COM

MOVEMENT FOR GLOBAL HEALTH

WITH DR. MARY ZENNETT

Doctor, Mom, and Global Health Advocate Passionate about improving the health status of individuals and communities.

Mission: To make our world a healthier place!

Dr. Mary has been a practicing psychiatrist for 35 years with Advanced training in Integrative Psychiatry and Lifestyle Medicine. She is now offering Holistic Mental Health consultation: **1)** as a Bioenergetics practitioner to help clear out energy blocks from emotions, past trauma, or the environment **2)** She works with adults and children with mental health conditions to stabilize on the most well-researched supplements in the world for mental health. **3)** Dr. Mary facilitates family workshops along with CARR 4Kids, the first series on children's self-esteem is coming up soon **4)** Dr. Mary also educates on healthy living on her Facebook page Mary Zennett. **5)** Her book on healthy eating and avoiding environmental toxins will be released soon

Dr. Mary Zennett is the Founder of Movement For Global Health and Podcast. Empowering individuals, activating communities, and compassion for the world. Together we can and will create a healthy world. Stay informed, stay empowered, and be well.

DR. MARY ZENNETT

Global Health Advocate, Speaker, Author and Podcaster

Biography

Hi I'm Dr. Mary Zennett. I empower real people who need to fine-tune their health and live life to the fullest. I've been a Board Certified Psychiatrist for 35 years and earned an Executive MBA in Health Administration. I am passionate about community health and transformation.

I also host a weekly podcast called "Movement For Global Health". If you are passionate about health, then you are going to love this show which brings together top speakers from the health and wellness industry with secrets to improve your quality of life.

Coming Soon!

This is a shopper's guide to healthy living! No need to guess anymore when you are in the grocery aisle or ordering online. Jam packed with lifestyle tips that can be life-saving for you and your family. Will be available on Amazon.

Interview Topics:

- Lessons we have Learned From COVID
- Our Mental Health Today: For Better or Worse
- Why Lifestyle Tips Are So Important
- Environmental Toxins: Eliminate the Damage!
- Health Secrets You Can Use Today

Interview questions:

- How did you become so passionate about health?
- Why are chronic illness rates so high in the US?
- Are there foods I should eat every day to stay healthy?
- How do I avoid exposure to toxins at home?
- As a society have we recovered from COVID?

Testimonial:

"Dr Mary is very knowledgeable and passionate about health and it is her mission to change the way the world looks at both physical and mental wellness." Arvee Robinson

Contact Dr Mary:

https://movementforglobalhealth.com

drmaryzennett@hushmail.com

WISDOM TIPS WITH DR. CONNIE GREEN

DR. CONNIE GREEN IS A LIFE COACH, CHRISTIAN COUNSELOR & HAS DEVOTED A GREAT DEAL OF HER LIFE TO HELPING WOMEN OVERCOME LIFE'S DISAPPOINTMENTS &; CHILDHOOD TRAUMA, THROUGH HEALTH & WELLNESS TO ACHIEVE MAXIMUM EMOTIONAL HEALTH

WISDOM TIPS

BY EXPERIENCING POSITIVE EMOTIONS TO INCREASE HAPPINESS THAT CAN CHANGE ATTITUDES BY LEARNED BEHAVIOR' AND ANYTHING THAT IS LEARNED CAN BE UNLEARNED. IF YOU ARE FACING A LIFE OF DISAPPOINTMENTS. JOIN US ON WISDOM TIPS WITH DR CONNIE GREEN HERE TO DROP PEARS OF TRUE WISDOM GIVING YOU THE TOOLS YOU NEED TO UNLOCK YOUR HAPPINESS, SO YOU CAN LIVE A VICTORIOUS LIFE.

SCAN ME

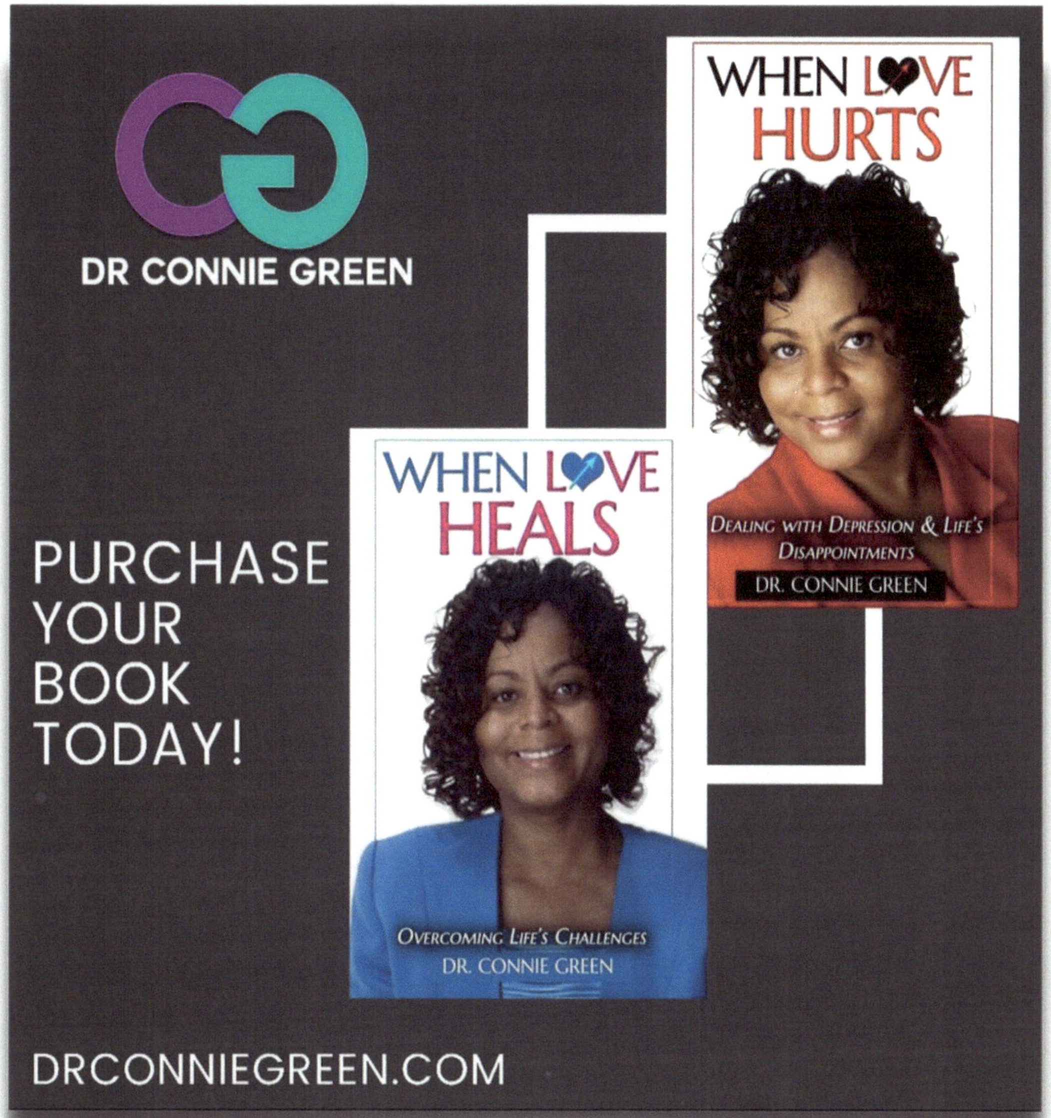

DR. CONNIE GREEN IS A LICENSED CHRISTIAN THERAPIST AND OFFERS COACHING ON VARIOUS LIFE SITUATIONS.

DR. CONNIE GREEN IS ONE OF THE NATION'S MOST REQUESTED SPEAKERS. DR. GREEN'S HONEST AND CANDID APPROACH TO MINISTRY HAS LANDED HER OPPORTUNITIES TO MINISTER TO THOUSANDS OF WOMEN ACROSS THE UNITED STATES. CONTACT US TODAY FOR INFORMATION REGARDING BOOKING DR. CONNIE GREEN FOR YOUR NEXT CONFERENCE, CONVENTION, RETREAT OR EVENT.

SCAN ME

THE MARLENE SAUNDERS SHOW& PODCAST

On this podcast you will always find something to fortify your mind, heal your heart, strengthen your convictions and give you the tools to live an abundant mindset and free spirit. A Florida content creator and podcaster. Welcome! This Podcast is all about Motivation, Inspiration, Life Lessons, and Positivity. On a day-to-day basis we go through things in our life. But the question is .. What is the quality of your life? Are you joyous? Have you been introduced to Worthiness, Forgiveness, Peace, Compassion, Fortitude?

"The Anna L. Brothers Podcast is about self-awareness, self-care, inspiring, encouraging and empowering people to live a healthy and better life."

Join me on my FB Lives weekly.

f **anna.brothers1**

📷 **annalassteen**

Anna L Brothers

Meet Anna L Brothers, your host for the "Anna L Brothers Show and Podcast". Join Anna, a retired schoolteacher and certified baker, as she shares her passion for leading a healthy lifestyle and taking care of oneself. With over 20 years of experience in decorating cakes with intricate icing designs and a love for hobbies such as knitting, jewelry making, sewing, and quilting, Anna has a lot to offer. As the owner of "The Jazzy Jewels Collections," Anna puts a little jazz in your step with her beautiful and affordable jewelry pieces, including her signature collection starting at just $25. With a passion for life and a desire to have fun, Anna is a divorced mother of one and proud grandmother to one granddaughter. Tune in every Wednesday at 7:30 PM CST for the live-streamed "Anna L Brothers Show and Podcast" where Anna covers topics on self-care and healthy living. Subscribe to her YouTube channel @annalbrothersshowandpodcastswe for even more inspiration and tips. Get ready to be inspired and add a little sparkle to your life with Anna L Brothers.

thejazzyjewelscollections.com
thejazzyjewelsboutique.com

My Total Life Changer Website
http://retail.totallifechanges.com/43143151

Deneen Consults

Deneen is a Passionate, Innovative, Executioner (P.I.E.) who leveraged years of program management, HR and leadership to launch Deneen Consults; consulting, coaching, speaking. She is also a podcaster, launched Women of Color: An Intimate Conversation in 2020, published author and active on several boards.

www.deneenconsults.com

WOMEN OF COLOR: AN INTIMATE CONVERSATION

DENEEN L. GARRETT

Pour Up Your Cup And Vibe On. Get Bodied With BossLadiStar Discuss Proper Planning And Enlightenment An Environment For Encouragement And Evolution.

Rev Up Your Back Office with TrueTMS

T3 Tech is a company of trucking technology experts driven by integrity and fueled by a passion to streamline the back office of small fleets. Mission accomplished.

TrueTMS is built expressly for the needs of small fleets. The modern, cloud-native platform has everything a small truckload carrier needs to simplify and automate the back office:

Order Lifecycle Management
Single-click functions to automate routine processes — rating loads, importing orders, tracking shipments, documenting deliveries, and more.

Load Planning and Dispatch
Quickly plan and assign loads to drivers with all the speed and power of an enterprise TMS, minus any unnecessary or distracting features. Mobile driver app captures load arrival, departure and other status details.

Driver Pay and Settlements
Automatically calculate driver payroll and settlements based on load mileage, percentage of revenue, and other user-defined scenarios.

On-Demand Reporting
User-friendly dashboards and customized reports to make faster, smarter decisions.

TrueTMS is continually expanding its offerings. Our agile development focuses on creating solutions and integrationsto to remove technology roadblocks for small fleets.

Get Up and Running Quickly
Implementing TrueTMS is a breeze. Your clunky spreadsheets and disjointed office tools will be in the rearview mirror — for good. The intuitive system trains users on the fly with a clean, fast, and sleek interface. Plus, all features and functions are well documented in a self-help menu.

Your Partner in Business

T3 Tech is more than a technology company. We invest in your success. Our trucking industry experts are creating a library of multi-media content to help you navigate the road ahead and make smarter, more profitable decisions.

Fully Connected

The responsive TrueTMS platform is always available, wherever you are, on any desktop, tablet, or mobile device. The platform connects with your chosen ELD telematics, accounting software, and other tools. We will continue to add new integrations and partnerships to further streamline and scale your business.

Connectivity options for TrueTMS currently include:

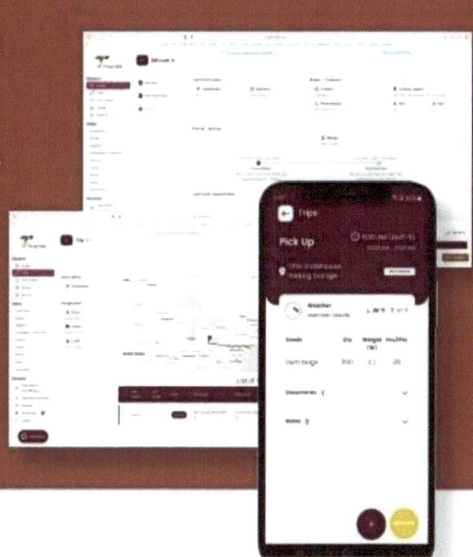

- More than 30 ELD and telematics providers. These integrations deliver real-time visibility of assets and driver hours to facilitate load planning, shipment tracking, and compliance, among other mission-critical processes.

- QuickBooks Online. Close the loop on freight transactions by exporting driver payroll, billing, and other financial data from TrueTMS.

- More integrations are coming. Do you have a specific need? **Let's talk.**

Start Your Free, No-Risk Trial

Don't take our word or settle for a demo. Go ahead – pop the hood and kick the tires. Experience TrueTMS for yourself with a 30-day free trial. No credit card is required.

Our pricing model is transparent with no contracts or hidden fees.

TrueTMS is fully independent of any other software or service. You will not receive sales pitches or have obligations to other vendors.

Visit **www.TrueTMS.com** to discover features and pricing tailored to small fleet success.

About T3 Tech

T3 Tech, LLC was founded in 2022 by a team of entrepreneurs. With headquarters in Melbourne, Fla., we are committed to meeting the technology needs of small fleet owners to help them grow and scale their businesses for the long haul.

SAFETY IN TRUCKING

Safety is of most importance in the trucking industry. Truck drivers must abide by the hours of service regulations to ensure they are not driving fatigued and have had adequate rest. They must also follow appropriate speed limits and be aware of their surroundings. It is important for truckers to practice defensive driving techniques, such as maintaining a safe following distance, and to inspect their vehicles regularly for any potential safety issues. Additionally, truckers should always wear their seatbelts and avoid distractions while driving. By following these tips and being mindful of their surroundings, truckers can ensure a safe journey.

Visit our website: www.shetrucking.com

S.H.E TRUCKING PODCAST was established in 2018 by Sharae Moore, a 10-year veteran professional truck driver. The podcast covers entrepreneurship, transportation topics, and lifestyle discussions. Tune in to listen to our transformational podcast on CTR MEDIA NETWORK. S.H.E. Trucking is Sponsored by: Relay Payment & TRUE TMS.

JOIN US!!

SHE Trucking

SHE TRUCKING ⓕ COMMUNITY

WWW.SHETRUCKING.COM

LEADERSHIP TEAM

Sharae Moore, Brand/Marketing Consultant, Author, and Founder of S.H.E. Trucking empowers more than 30,000 women and minorities in the transportation industry.

Sharae has been a professional driver since 2014 and her advocacy work has been recognized by various organizations and media outlets, including: The White House, Facebook, National Geographic - Breaking Bobby Bones: Ep.7 Truck Star, CNN - 2021 Champion for Change, National Truckin' Magazine - Legend Driver, and has received the Trucking Industry Trailblazer Award for Diversity and Inclusion.

Thank you to our leadership team's exceptional leadership and unwavering commitment to empowering women in the trucking industry. Your, dedication, and tireless efforts have not only created a supportive community but also inspired countless individuals to pursue their dreams fearlessly. Thank you for breaking barriers, fostering inclusivity, and advocating for positive change.

Transenergy CDL Academy

Age Requirement
18 and Older
CALL US TODAY TO START YOUR TRUCKING CAREER!
(704) 614 - 6540

LIMITED SPACES AVAILABLE

Job Placement Available
Course Fee Includes :

**Classroom Materials,
Behind The Wheel Training
And MVR.**

📍 Located in Eastridge Mall Upstairs Next To Curt's:
246 N. New Hope Rd.,Gastonia, NC 28054

Enroll Today!
www.transenergycdlacademy.com
(704) 614 - 6540

Payment Arrangements Available

As a woman-owned institution, they are dedicated to providing top-notch training and support for aspiring truck drivers. Transenergy CDL Academy is an ideal choice for women seeking to enter the trucking industry. We I highly recommend Transenergy CDL Academy as a trusted trucking school that aligns with the values and goals of SHE Trucking.

82

HISRAY PUBLISHING
Shana Asby

START FROM
$49.99
PER ITEM

Manual Content
BOOK CREATING/PUBLISHING
$999.99-$1499
MAGAZINE
$299.99&UP
BIO/PRESS KITS
$149.99

Digital E-Book
LOGO
$49.99&UP
DIGITAL FLYER
$49.99&UP
DIGITAL MAGAZINE COVER
$99.99

Project Management
NON-PROFIT
$199&UP
PODCASTS
$299.99&UP
VISIONARY STARTER
$49.99&UP
PHOTOGRAPHY
$49.99 AN HOUR
DIGITAL E-BOOK
$999-1299
VIDEO SLIDE PROMOTION
$99.99

CONTACT US
HisRAy Publishing
Shana Asby
HisRayPublishing@gmail.com

1+803-670-6736

83
PODCAST REVOLUTION MAGAZINE

Business Spotlight

Tamara Dopwell

As a social entrepreneur, Tee has over 15 years of medical social work experience and currently works in space of ElderJustice. Tee has utilized her creativity to create a socially-conscious T-shirt line. Designs by Tee is purposeful and strategic in working with corporations, non-profit leaders, faith-based organizations, social workers and educators to enhance their organizations' goals.

DBT's core value is reaching the unreached through essential toiletries. Each purchase provides a local homeless family the dignity of having what they need. Since Covid has placed new challenges, she continues to further her work. She wants her customers to look good with their Tee but more importantly, feel good, knowing their purchase is enhancing Social Justice.

SCAN ME

Designs By Tee

A podcast on Education, Leadership, Enrichment, Empowerment & Wellbeing

With a purposeful career in the education space spanning over more than 20 years, PROF. (DR.) SHAULI MUKHERJEE has dedicated her life towards promotion of child-centric and activity-oriented education. A passionate educationist and a global thought leader with a background of setting up and leading new age K- 12 schools, Dr. Mukherjee had been the Founder Principal of Adamas World School and STEM World School, the first STEM school in West Bengal. Under her inspiring leadership, STEM World School had been ranked and awarded as the 2nd best International Day School in West Bengal by Education World. Dr. Mukherjee has also held senior academic and administrative positions in some of the reputed colleges of West Bengal.

PROF. DR. SHAULI MUKHERJEE, INDIA
CTR MEDIA NETWORK INTERNATIONAL PODCASTER

She ardently believes that the purpose of meaningful education is to develop lifelong learners, creative thinkers and responsible global citizens who are confidently equipped to face the challenges of an uncertain and constantly unfolding future. All through her career in education, Dr. Mukherjee had actively contributed to and spearheaded the process of creating a personalized, engaging and stress-free curriculum for learners of all age groups. She has been the recipient of numerous awards and accolades including NATIONAL QUALITY EXCELLENCE AWARD, GEM OF INDIA AWARD, SARVEPALLI RADHAKRISHNAN AWARD, NATIONAL EDUCATION LEADERSHIP AWARD in the category of commitment to excellence in education, WORLD PEACE AWARD (to name a few).

INDIA

She has also been awarded for being among India's Top 50 Women Leaders in the Education Industry and Top 20 Revolutionary Education Leaders by the Academic Council of ULektz. She is associated with premiere educational organizations across India as well as globally in senior advisory capacity. She is also recognized among 99 Women Achievers of India for the year 2021. She has been listed among the Top 50 Most Courageous Women in Business, Leadership and Entertainment in 2022. As an internationally acclaimed inspirational speaker, she is regularly invited to numerous national and international conferences, universities, summits, conclaves and events to share her insights on the futuristic and transformative role of education. She is currently working as the Director of School of Education and Associate Dean - School of Liberal Arts and Culture Studies at Adamas University, India.

PROF. DR. SHAULI MUKHERJEE, INDIA

By Host Tatia Bradley

Love yourself' Be yourself 'and most of all Stay True Yourself. My name is Tatia Bradley Host of Daily Dose of Love with Tatia. Welcome to the Tribe/ Self Love Club, Where I'm Encouraging Self-Love through Self-Care. Self-love is so underrated Make it a Priority in your Life, and Treat it as Such. Tune in Each and Every Wednesday for New Episode's wherever you Podcast!! Self -Love is the Best Love!! Thanks for your Ear Time Ilove always.See less

Listen on SpotifySupport this podcastSend voice message

Listen on

APARTMENTS ONLY

Need a Move-out Clean??

KNOWLEDGABLE. EXPERIENCED. DETAILED

1 Bedroom	2 Bedroom	3 Bedroom
$99	$115	$120

AVOID THOSE CLEANING FEES MANAGEMENT CHARGE

844-656-8359
HTTPS://CLEAN4ME.INFO/

Services in South Carolina & Surrounding Areas

Why your mind dislikes change, and what to instantly do about it?

Have you ever been excited about making changes in your life? You begin feeling a rush of energy and a sense of hope and excitement.

Then, that familiar voice in your head kicks in, making you afraid to try anything new. Unfortunately, your brain believes you are limited in what you can do. It sees anything that is unfamiliar as a potential threat-even if it's something you want to do! It just wants to be efficient in protecting you, so it holds you back.

Feeling uncomfortable, you begin to doubt your decision to try something new. Next, because familiarity feels safer than making changes, you tell yourself it's better to do nothing. And how you justify doing nothing is by telling yourself the original situation you wanted to change wasn't so bad. It's not so bad tolerating that toxic relationship, feeling unhealthy or overworking. And then you engage in wishful thinking again and the cycle repeats.

SCAN ME

Elizabeth Harper Coaching

ELIZABETHHARPERCOACHING.COM

Perhaps you're thinking about starting a podcast (trigger), you feel scared and distract yourself (routine) and don't start one (result). When repeated enough times, your brain will automatically focus on distracting yourself and less on making changes.

Repeatedly responding to a trigger in the same way makes your brain focus away from your original goal and more on how you respond And if your reaction is unhelpful, you'll find yourself getting further away from your original plan. Crazy, right?

So, habitual thoughts are controlled by the subconscious mind and tend to become unconscious, automatic, and normal to us. And we rarely question what has become normal, but we should. Because most of our decisions are based on our negative mindset. And we are training our minds to automatically think and believe the same thoughts daily, whether true or false, encouraging or disruptive. And to respond the same way.

Please understand you cannot always trust your thoughts and feelings, especially if they are habitual. You need to get out of autopilot, and it takes repeated consistent practice. But this takes time, so what can you do now?

Begin by paying attention to your habitual thoughts and reactions when it comes to making changes. If you feel scared, disrupt the feeling and pattern by doing something physical such as clapping or taking a small action step toward your goal, like doing research.

Think of your negative habitual mindset as a separate persona and give it a name. Naming it will remind you that it's not necessarily who you are and allows you to view it from a rational perspective.

Right now, start thinking from the mindset of someone who has done what you want to do. How would they think or feel, and what would they do? Part of the problem is making changes from a self-image that thinks we are limited, and you are going to consistently think and behave as who you believe yourself to be. If you believe you are not capable, you'll never try anything new. Believe that you are.

Elizabeth Harper is on a mission helping women exchange wishful thinking for successful living. As a certified life coach, she transforms self-doubters into confident manifesters ™. Her course "Confident You Makeover" helps women achieve their unique self-image and life. Elizabeth is also an author featured in numerous magazines and media.

The Introduction to Podcasting
WHO AM I?

Allow me to introduce myself. I am Shamiya Woodard, A bail bondsman born in the Bronx but raised as a country girl in a small town called Ridgeway, South Carolina. I am a single mother of three wonderful children. They're the reason WHY I decided to become an entrepreneur. My mission is to build a better bail bonding company with the core value of being the fastest, friendliest, most affordable, passionate, and professional in the state. Although I only serve six countries, I aim to build a team big enough and strong enough to serve the entire state and my few others. Passionate about my business, I was seeking ways to get more recognition so that I could connect with other individuals who may want to learn more about the industry and want to join the growth.

Has podcasting been on your list of things to do? Well, guess what, it is possible. Do you know what podcasts are? A podcast is a digital audio, essentially a talk radio series on demand. This means that listeners can listen at any time, any place, and it tends to focus on a theme or topic. For most listeners, podcasts are a way to enjoy great content for free worldwide.

Shamiya Woodard

Hello, I'm Shamiya Woodard, a Bail Bondswoman from South Carolina. Looking for ways to tell my story and expand my business, I had my first introduction to podcasting and the joy of interviewing for one at an event called "Closing the Gap" in Columbia, South Carolina. Days Prior to this event, I was googling and on YouTube trying to figure out how I could get someone to interview me on their podcast. How can I get my story out? And God places me at this event. I went home and decided since I was late, I wasn't going to bother going. God kept saying go. So finally, I contacted coach Nakeisha and asked if one more ticket was available. She said just come. Getting to the event for the last two hours, I went to sit in the corner just to listen in and learn what I could. I was the last one to get there, so when it was time to spin the wheel to win the prize, I was the one picked to do it. The funny thing is I was hiding because I'm not good with crowds. I try not to be in a place where I will get picked to participate or talk. I just prefer to listen and take notes.

But usually, when I do talk people enjoy the conversation. So, as I gently spent the wheel, I won a podcast interview with CTR Media Network. Can you say nervous but excited? After winning I was told to go to Mrs. Tina to be interviewed. My heart was overwhelmed. When I got to the back where they were set up, her husband was packing up. He smiled, and with a friendly, calm voice, he said, "your right on time. Go tell my wife we need to interview you. As I waited her husband had me sit in the interview chair and set up everything. Mrs. Tina didn't hesitate. She came and sat by me, asking a few questions before we aired. She instructed me on how to introduce myself and my business. While talking to her and her husband it was hard to be nervous. They talked as if we'd known each other for years. I have been to many events but never experienced anything as such. Mrs. Tina introduced her podcast to me, told me how the interview would go, and walked me through step by step. She made it so easy to do.

Once the camera started she did the introduction with ease. She was so calm and her smile brightened the room. I couldn't help but be calm too. The podcast interview was as simple as conversing normally while holding a microphone. Yes, they made it just that simple. As the interview began Mrs. Tina asked the questions quickly so that in between her talking and asking questions, there was no room for anxiety or nervousness. I must say for the first time meeting her and her husband and the first time being interviewed, it was an AMAZING EXPERIENCE. If you are interested in starting a podcast or if you just desire to be interviewed on one, CTR MEDIA NETWORK is the place. The CTRMN team are such beautiful people and the work they are doing is great. Making so many differences in the world by reaching 350 million households worldwide in over 50 countries, they're really making a huge impact, and to think they allowed me the opportunity to be a part is a blessing. Giving small businesses like me a chance to use their platform is awesome.

We appreciate it. With a family-like atmosphere, warm welcome, and down-to-earth heart, Mrs. Tina and her husband are amazing people to connect with. I enjoyed every moment, from meeting them to being interviewed by them. The experience was nothing short of amazing. I thank God for allowing me to be late and still blessing me with the opportunity to work with such amazing people. During the interview, I was taught to speak confidently, don't think too hard, and flow with the person interviewing me, and things will go smoothly. CTR MEDIA NETWORK has allowed me to become what I would consider a part of their family. Not letting you go empty-handed, after interviewing, they exchanged all social media platforms and gave many tips about podcasting, advice on getting your business heard and seen, and words of encouragement. Mrs. Tina gives you her undivided attention and assures you that she will be willing to help you expand and that her platform is not just for her but for the growth of everyone she meets. I would love to do an interview again. Thank you, CTR MEDIA NETWORK, for such an amazing opportunity. Continue to make a difference. Your hard work isn't unnoticed.

Featured

THE

Tina Ramsay

SHOW

Shamiya Woodard

Mobile Notary
Credit Repair
Tax Services
24 Hour Bail Bonds

Ms. Rapid Release

DR,. UMAR JOHNSON
SEASON:1 EPOSIDE:

The Men Can't Always Be Wrong Podcast provides a weekly conversation from a male point of view on current events, finances, health issues, and relationships. If you want insight into what men are thinking. Tune in with J. Bean, Stevon, LDC1, and T Swin, because men can't always be wrong.

Steve-O.

TSwin

JBean

LDC1

MEN THOUGHTS PODCAST is where men discuss business, well-being, mental health, money, fatherhood, relationships, and more. You will be able to gain different men's perspectives about life and its journey. You will be introduced to various standout men making an impact to help men and young boys grow into manhood by sharing their experiences.

This podcast is seeking Co-Host. Go to **CTRMediaNetwork.com** to learn more.

THE HOMESCHOOLING INTERACTIVE MAGAZINE

Impacting the World Through Home-Based Learning

CTR MEDIA NETWORK

SPECIAL MENTAL HEALTH EDITION

Joy Inside Tears

MENTAL HEALTH CHALLENGES AND DISORDERS IN CHILDREN AND YOUTH

7 PROVEN TIPS

FOR A THRILLING START TO YOUR HOMESCHOOLING JOURNEY

BEST MATH CURRICULA FOR SPECIAL NEEDS CHILDREN

Featuring

ORDER NOW

"THESE DRY BONES" AUTHOR & EDUCATOR

ESTEE "E DOT" MARIE

SCAN ME

THEQUEENCANDI
Podcast

My show is where I talk about every topic under the sun and nothing is left off limits!! My show is for the ladies. I empower and uplift all my queens to be better and to let them know they can follow their dreams!!

CTR MEDIA NETWORK

PODCAST PRODUCTION & DISTRIBUTION

CTR MEDIA NETWORK is a new standard of podcasting, **reaching 350M+ households in 100+ countries** across major podcast streaming platforms. We help podcasters and entrepreneurs to grow and maximize their visibility and brand through The Power Of Podcasting.

Spotify · Listen on Apple Podcasts

  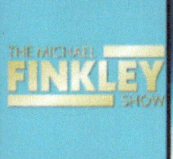     

FOR MORE INFORMATION:
SCAN HERE

CTR MEDIA OFFERS:

- PODCAST PRODUCTION
- PODCAST TRAINING
- PHOTOGRAPHY
- PRODUCT PLACEMENT
- INTERVIEWS
- AD PLACEMENTS
- COMMERCIAL SLOTS
- SPONSORSHIP OPP.

      TUNE IN  iHeart RADIO

 CTR MEDIA NETWORK PODCASTERS JOIN NOW

 WWW.CTRMEDIANETWORK.COM **CTRMEDIANETWORK1@GMAIL.COM**

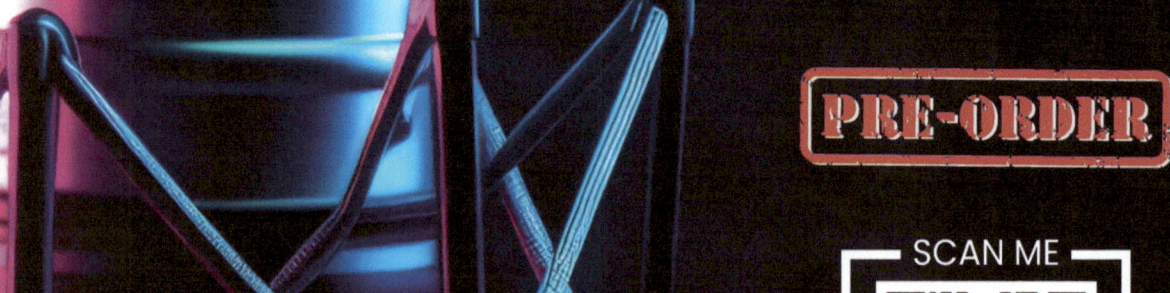

The Power of AI
PODCAST

Coming Soon

PRE-ORDER

SCAN ME

Dr. Tina J Ramsay

SHIRLEY RUMPH

Safe Hearts Book Selection

ON A MISSION TO EMPOWER WOMEN, CHILDREN, AND MEN WITH SAFETY

Featured THE *Tina Ramsay* SHOW

My name is Shirley Riley Rumph. I am on a mission to empower women, children, and men with safety. I am proud to be an independent representative of Damsel. In defense, my goal is to educate and bring awareness to how we can help protect ourselves and our families. I would love the chance to share our mission and products with you. Also, being a grandmother of three grandsons, I am super excited about our safety health collection books which bring knowledge to your children.

SAFE Hearts stands for Sharing Awareness for Family Empowerment. This family education line is designed to help adults and children navigate the most important, yet difficult conversations; to empower children to take ownership over their own hearts and bodies, raise their awareness, and give them the ability to protect themselves against anyone who may try to harm them.

This educational line focuses on prevention just as much as it does on healing and restoration. Learn more or download free resources at safehearts.com

SAFE HEARTS BOOK SELECTION

101

You can Homeschool your children and be successful at doing it with the proper resources and community. We help you destress the Homeschooling Experience.

This podcast provides Homeschooling Tips, Resources, Reviews and more to support you on your Homeschooling and Life Journey. You will also be introduced to various educators , services, products, and speakers on this podcast through Guest Co-Host.

HOMESCHOOLING HELP

Melanated Homeschooling Families Podcast provide a safe place for Black & Brown Homeschoolers to come together to connect, communicate, and introduce you to some amazing Melanated Homeschoolers from all over the world. We will share information to help easer the stress of homeschooling with the supportive community you need. We will discuss various topics centered around Homeschool, Business, Wellness and Life for our perspective.

THE EDU-STATION STORE

"The EDU-Station Store, Where We Make Learning Fun."

Our mission is simple:
"Make every daycare owner's business more profitable by providing them with quality yet affordable and reusable educational materials they can use in any curriculum."

The EDU-Station store is located at 1200 N. Holtzclaw Ave Chattanooga, Tennessee founded by LaShon Carter. The EDU-Station store offers a variety of student and teacher educational materials, lamination services, and the Let's Go Kit subscription boxes at a low cost to childcare providers. The EDU-Station Store: Let's Go Kit is the only subscription box designed perfect for Educators, Parents, Schools, Camps, Churches, Afterschool programs, and Childcare providers looking to educate their children from ages 1-5.

MATERIALS THAT BOOST IMAGINATION AND ENCOURAGE FUN WHILE LEARNING

The EDU-Station Store also offers workbooks aligned with the Early Learning and Development Standards. All workbooks are filled with age-appropriate worksheets, coloring pages, and hands-on activities. These activities will help children develop their fine motor skills, cognitive abilities, and problem-solving skills while having fun.

"My kids enjoy the worksheets from the books plus it doesn't seem like the kids are working because we are having so much fun."

Latasha Knight, Owner of Tiny Tada Daycare

In this issue,

LaShon Carter is also the owner of Tiny Tigers Learning Center. Tiny Tigers Learning Center provides quality care to the community at an affordable price. Our goal is to prepare your child for elementary school.

The EDU-Station Store is also available online. To learn more about the EDU-Station Store visit their website:

www.letsgoexpress.org

103

THE IMPORTANCE OF HASHTAGS FOR PODCASTING

By Curtis Ramsay

Hashtags can be important for podcasting because they can help increase visibility and discoverability of your podcast.

When you use hashtags in your podcast episode titles, descriptions, and social media posts, it can make it easier for people to find your content when they are searching for topics related to your podcast.

Hashtags can also help you to reach a wider audience beyond your existing followers. When people search for a particular hashtag, they may come across your podcast and discover your content for the first time.

"USING HASHTAGS STRATEGICALLY CAN BE A VALUABLE FOR PODCASTERS"

In addition, using relevant and popular hashtags can also help you to join conversations and communities around particular topics. This can help you to engage with listeners and potential listeners, and build relationships with others in your niche.

Overall, using hashtags strategically can be a valuable way to increase the visibility and reach of your podcast, and to connect with new and existing audiences.

THE GEO MONROE SHOW & PODCAST

**Motivation, Home Biz,
Affiliate Marketing,
& Friends with Super Channels**
LET'S GET THIS SHOW MOVING

GEO'S MAIN WEBSITE: HTTPS://GEOANDMONROE.COM

The Geo Monroe Show and Podcast will Interview YouTube Content Creators about their channel or Channels.

Let's Get Chatty with different various topics.

SCAN ME

LEARN HOW TO MONETIZE YOUR YOUTUBE CHANNEL

◀ Learn Math Fast

The Learn Math Fast System is different from your typical curriculum. Are your math skills rusty or non-existent? No problem, just stay one lesson ahead of your child and you can teach math while you learn it at the same time.

SCAN ME

Use Code: **HSOILS** and save 10%

Rated 5 -Stars by The Homeschooling Magazine

The Homeschooling Magazine Podcast is an extension of our magazine to impact the world through Home Based Learning. This podcast and YouTube Channel will provide Homeschooling Tips, Resources, Reviews and more to support you on your Homeschooling and Life Journey.

Peek Inside Volume 1 of This Curriculum Before you Buy It.

SCAN ME

To Watch the Video

SUBSCRIBE

Please Subscribe and Like our YouTube Channel

The Sheila C. Hill Show is the ultimate go-to podcast for ambitious individuals who want to live a more fulfilling and successful life. Join your host Sheila C. Hill, to acquire valuable insights, expert tips, and inspiring stories to help you improve your lifestyle, grow your business, and enhance your emotional being. In every episode, you'll gain practical tips and insightful wisdom in the company of a supportive community of like-minded individuals. Tune in every week for your dose of motivation and inspiration. Let's grow together!

I read "The Power of Podcasting " during the day and even when it's lights out. To keep from disturbing my husband. I put on my headlight and keep reading and studying. This book is in a class of its on! I love it! ❤

Sheila C. Hill

PODCAST REVOLUTION MAGAZINE 107

BEAUTY FOR ASHES
PODCAST

Beauty for Ashes is a Selfcare, Mental Health Awareness and Wellness Podcast that encourages, empowers and enlightens listeners on how to create wellness and develop strategies for a healthier mindset.

joyinsidetears IG
joyinsidetears FB

Email: info@joyinsidetears.com

Joy Inside Tears Non-profit Organization provides mental health and suicide prevention resources, support, advocacy, counseling, and educational training throughout the greater Georgia area. Help us fight to end the stigma associated with mental health.

THE VERA THOMAS SHOW

The **Vera Thomas Show** is a weekly show live on Tuesdays and Thursdays at 7pm EST. It is designed to uplift, encourage, motivate, inspire and educate. Poetry is shared!

Vera is a Certified Life Coach and Classroom Management Consultant, International Speaker, Trainer, Mediator, Poet and 16x Best Selling Author. She has worked with individuals, companies, non-profit organizations, schools, and churches engaging youth and adults for over 30 years. Vera's life experiences have given her purpose and passion to make a difference in the lives of children as well as adults.

KATHY GREGGS

● ● ●

Fayetteville Police Accountability Community Taskforce

Kathy Greggs was born in Camden, New Jersey. She grew up in Germany. Her mother and father retired and served in the United States Army, which is where she followed their traditions. As a US Army Combat Veteran, and military sexual assault survivor; her advocacy in the US Army helping change the US Army policy and procedures with reporting and discharging for emotional trauma victims. Her personal experience led to volunteering at Connections of Cumberland where she did case management for homeless women and children. She is a certified FEMA Disaster Operations Manager who coordinated relief efforts during Hurricane Irma, Matthew, Florence in NC and Hurricane Harvey and Wildfire Thomas in California. Served as a co-advocate, for Pathway to Prosperity housing to assist those out of poverty. She served as the Chair for City of Fayetteville Board of Commissioners, for Public Arts.

Black Women Rising on Police Accountability.

MAKING A DIFFERENCE

She is the Co-founder of Fayetteville Police Accountability Community Taskforce; a nonprofit organization that seeks to change statewide and national regulations, policies, and laws within the criminal justice system. Fayetteville PACT also address any racial injustices no matter what race, gender, sexual orientation, religion. She assisted with the write up on SB 682 with Senator DeViere, on establishing Citizen Review Boards at all cities and municipalities across NC.

Greggs led or served on several civil rights and civil liberties organizations. She formerly served as the North Carolina Director and Military Liaison for the Domestic Violence Rally, Board of Directors for NewLife2nd Chances, Governance Committee Board for ACLU of NC, Steering Committee for Sheriff Trusting Communities, Vice President for NC National Organizing of Women Legislation Action. She is currently Board of Directors for Pro-Choice NC, Board Member At-Large of Fayetteville Pride, NC Climate Ambassador.

She believes that all communities including the disenfranchised and demarginalized need infrastructure for sustainability and government agencies should not leave them behind.

Greggs holds a Master of Business Administration in Human Resource Management from Columbia Southern University and is currently seeking a PhD in Theology. She is a recipient of North Carolina A. Philip Randolph Institute " Community Leader Award" 2022. Juneteenth Freedom Pioneer Award (2019), Presidential Volunteer Service Bronze Award (2018), "I Care Award" from Cumberland County for Volunteer Service (2017).

www.fayettevillepact.com
kathygreggsspeaks@gmail.com

TANYA D. HAITHCOCK, M.A.

Find The Words

Case Manager
Peer Recovery Support Specialist

Whether it be mental illness, substance abuse, survival of sex abuse or domestic abuse, if you are in a Recovery Program and are not comfortable expressing your feelings and talking about your issues because of fear of judgement or lack of trustworthy support you will not get well. The right support is important! Finding a good fit with care providers can be frustrating. I may be able to help because I was a client.

Using Mindfulness and Creativity along with the client's clinical plan as a means of going through the journey of recovery, I have been successful in becoming that support and guidance needed. I have also lived these experiences myself. I have been in "That Life" and have a personal understanding of the struggle. I have been living in recovery for fourteen years.

My background is in the Dramatic Arts, Writing and Social Services. I have spent twenty years working as a Case Manager with various agencies offering care in the most underserved populations of Chicago, Illinois, Winston Salem and Greensboro North Carolina, and Lima, Ohio. ·As Case Manager and Peer Recovery Support Specialist I assess the client's physical and mental wellness, living needs, and abilities, and work directly with the client, their family and health care professionals to put Recovery plans in place.

- I provide education, mentoring, informal counselling or intervention as required.
- I Follow the client's progress through interaction, performance in meetings, home visits, etc. Progress and Outcomes will be documented.
- Advocate for the client's wellbeing.
- I am a living, breathing, broken and rebuilt example of someone who lives one moment at a time in Recovery, and I present my personal experience of how I use treatment, Mindfulness and Creativity to STAY in Recovery.
- I maintain a high standard of personal conduct and respect the rights and individuality of others.

YOU FIND THE WORDS AND SAY SO!
"I WANT TO BE FREE!"
(773) 354-0310

Purchase our Products!

www.CtrMediaNetwork.com

PODCAST REVOLUTION MAGAZINE

BUTTERCON MAGAZINE

 **MAGAZINE TOPICS:**

WHO ARE WE?

ButterCon Magazine is a contemporary publication offering stories, articles, expert advice and advertisements that's relatable to all from every day people, regarding every day life.

WHAT WE DO?

ButterCon Magazine started in 2020 during Covid representing 8 states with stories, articles and advertisements. We have now grown to over 23 states and have thus far published 10 quarterly editions.

CONTACT US FOR INFORMATION ON WRITING AND ADVERTISING:

 803-989-7820

 kymlahburton@butterconmagazine.com

 www.butterconmagazine.com

Amen Corner
Today's Entrepreneur
Cuisine
Hair Story
ShopTalk
The Conversation Piece
The AuthoR's Place
Health
Wellness
Real Estate/
What's Happening In The
Neighborhood
Money Matters
Entertainment
Advertising

SPECIAL EDITIONS:

Twice a year ButterCon Magazine will have publications with stories, articles, advertising for walks, events, as well as fundraisers to bring awareness to crime, health issues, special needs, diseases and other information that affect our everyday lives.

PODCAST REVOLUTION MAGAZINE

KEARN CHERRY

Speaker, coach, 22x #1 best-selling author, and award-winning businesswoman Kearn Crockett Cherry is a female tycoon with a "leg-up" in successful entrepreneurship. Laying to rest any stigma surrounding the stagnancy of female leadership in the Deep South, Kearn has enjoyed more than twenty-five years of excellence as co-owner of PRN Home Care. She is often called the "Visibility Queen" and "Butts in the Seats Queen."

Kearn hosts a portfolio holding countless awards, acknowledging her abilities; locally, nationally, and internationally. She is a recognized figure in both business and communal leadership, holding membership and chair positions on diverse councils and local organizations.

The Success Women's Conference is an award winning-business leadership conference attracting an annual audience of over 17,000 attendees worldwide. Kearn Cherry and her contributing partners has a reputation for revolutionizing the way women interpret both public speaking and business, on a global scale. Kearn is also the creator of two innovative virtual conferences; "Level-Up Virtual Summit" and "Power Up Summit" which are both international events. Through her KKonnections, she assist clients in creating their own profitable events and increasing their visibility.

In 2001, Kearn Cherry effortlessly graced the pages of one of the most popular publications in the world, Essence Magazine. Featured in both their local, and international publications; Kearn was recognized as the "Comeback Queen", confirming her commitment to exemplifying dynamic business agility. Today, Kearn is a familiar face on several Magazine covers. Recently featured on Black Enterprise, VIP Magazine, Speakers Magazine, Sheen Magazine, and her very own, are among her favorites.

"Butts in the Seats Queen."

Featured THE *Tina Ramsay* SHOW

Giving birth to Amazon's #1 best-selling book; Trailblazers Who Lead: Unsung Heroes, a manuscript comprising 29 stories featuring several well-respected female entrepreneurs, moguls, and business professionals.

Enthusiastic about the future, Kearn remains diligent in helping entrepreneurs reach their destined potential. She recently released a #1 Bestseller - "Make It Happen" anthology with 30 authors. She is the visionary for "Trailblazers Who Lead II" and the latest bestselling anthology "Undefeated" - women sharing their secrets to winning.

KKonnections

www.kearncherry.com

PODCAST EVENTS

SCAN ME

PODCAST EVENTS

The Power of Podcasting Event: A podcasting event in Marietta, Georgia, teaching about podcasting, networking, entertainment, motivation, and experience being apart of a LIVE tapping of The Tina Ramsay Show powered by CTR Media Network.

5th Anniversary Afros & Audio Podcast Festival is a community of independent podcasters dedicated to curating accessible/inclusive events and spaces for and by Black Podcast Creatives & Audio Professionals.

Podcast Movement: an annual conference and trade show for podcasters and the podcast industry, which started in 2014, it is considered the largest of its kind in the world.

Black Effect Podcast Network
WHERE BLACK THOUGHTS LIVE!

The Podcast Academy and The Podcast Awards: an annual ceremony held in the US.

Podfest: A big annual event in the US.

She Podcasts Event: A podcasting event for women and non-binary people.

Podcast MidAtlantic: Podcasting event in the mid-Atlantic region of the US.

Podcast Day: A global virtual event for podcasters and podcast industry professionals

The Podcast Upfront: A virtual event for advertisers and podcast creators to come together to discuss the business of podcast.

The Black Podcasters Association
Uniting Black podcast creatives and professionals committed to redefining the podcast landscape through community.

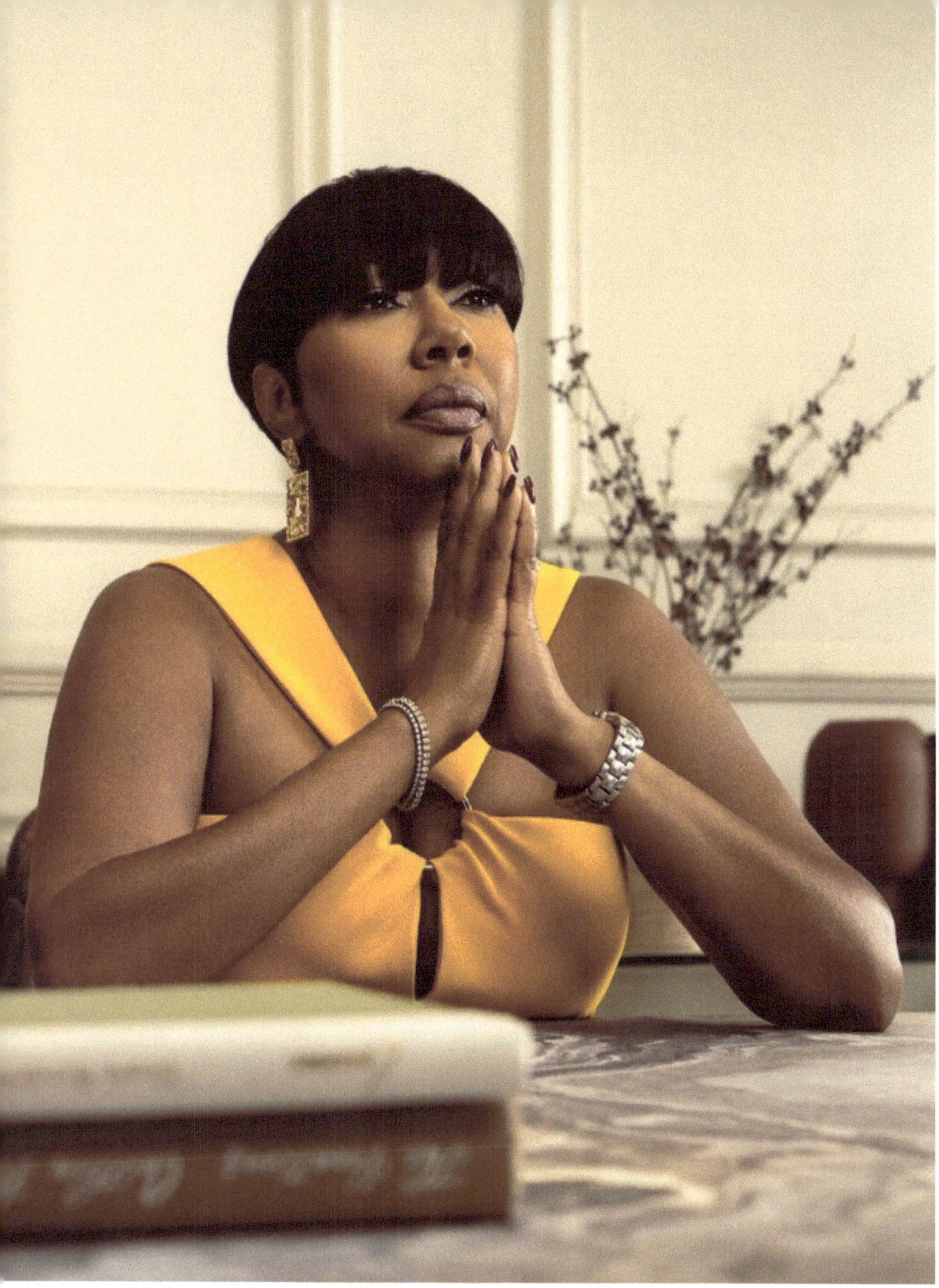

DR. TINA J. RAMSAY

ON AIR
MEN

CTR MEDIA
NETWORK
Stop Your Leaky Gut!
with
ALUVA

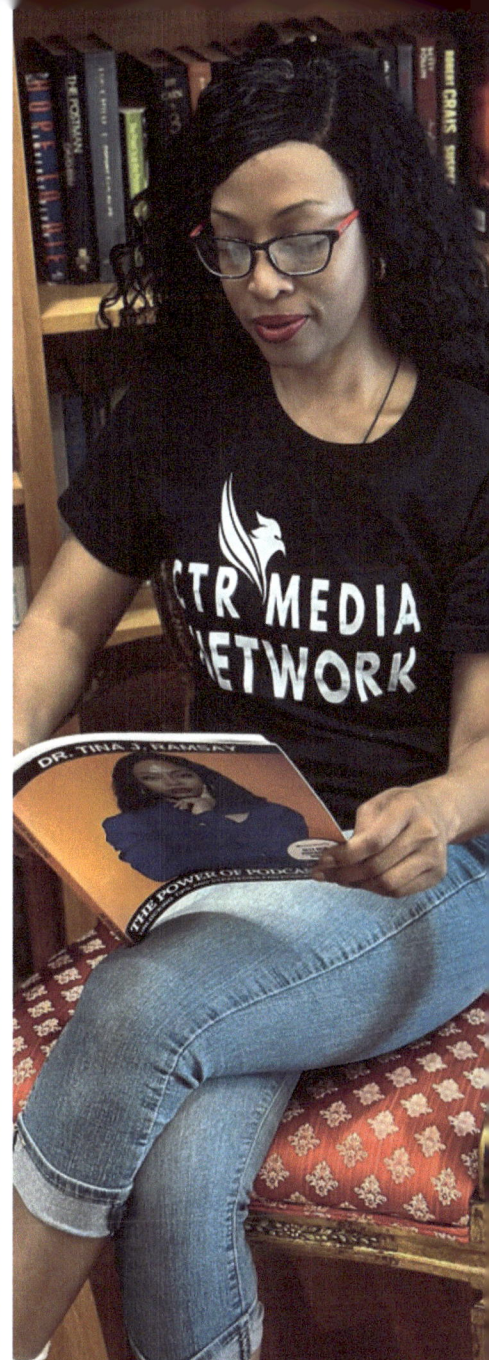

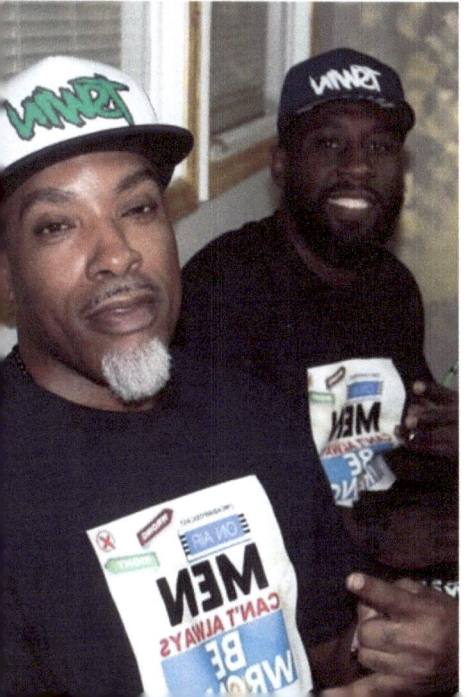

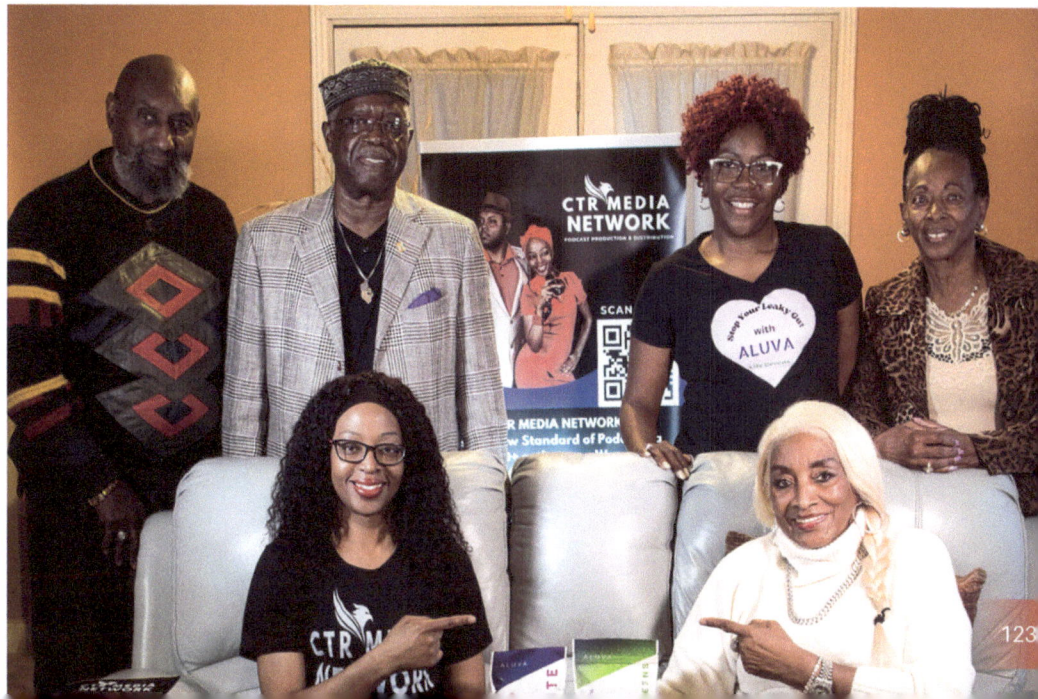

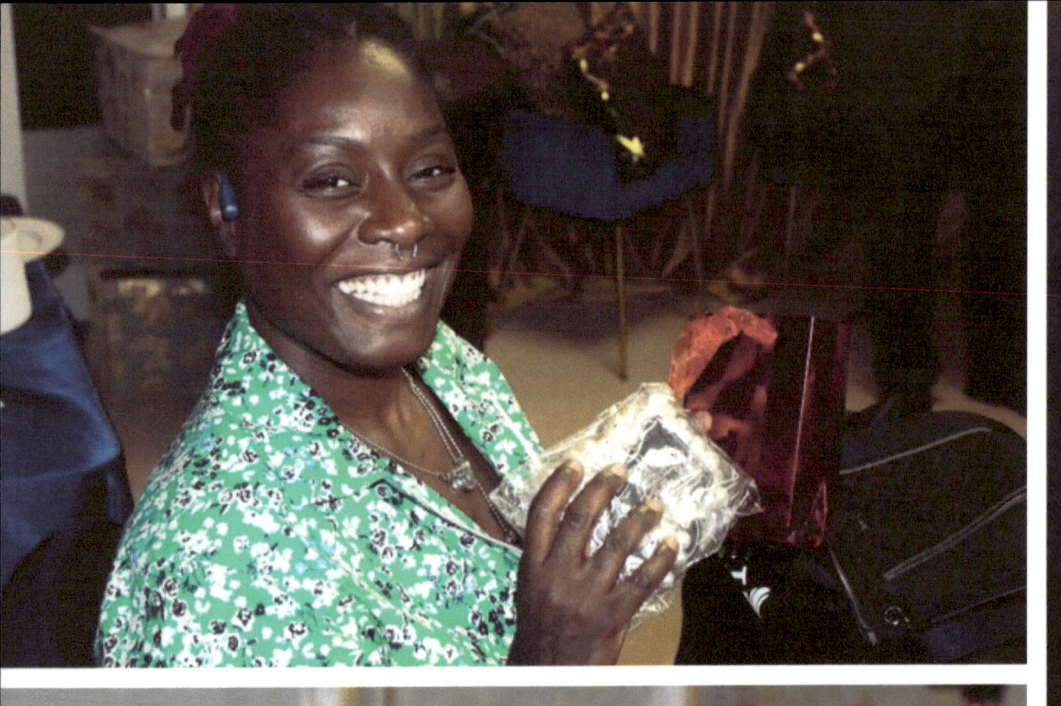

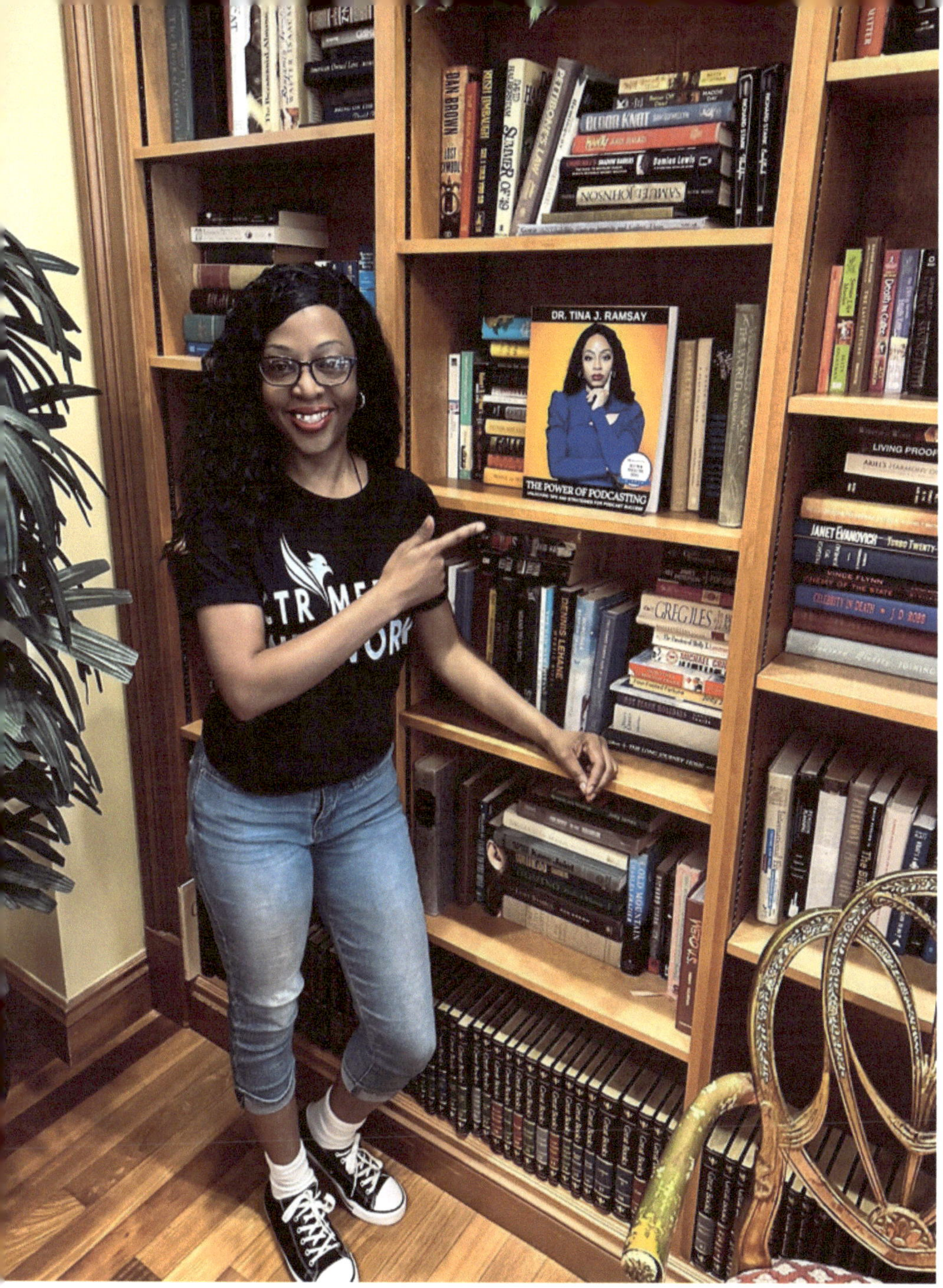
DR. TINA J. RAMSAY
THE POWER OF PODCASTING
DAN BROWN
SAMUEL JOHNSON
LIVING PROOF
JANET EVANOVICH
VINCE FLYNN
CELEBRITY IN DEATH
J. D. ROBB
GREG ILES
DENNIS LEHANE

Legacy

CTR MEDIA
NETWORK
PODCASTERS
JOIN NOW

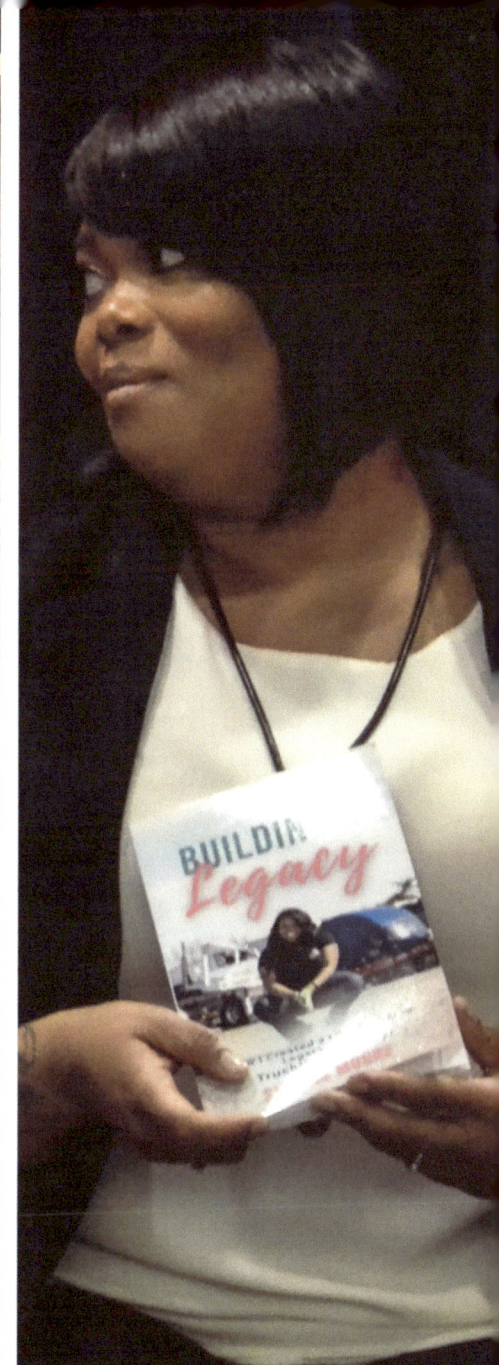

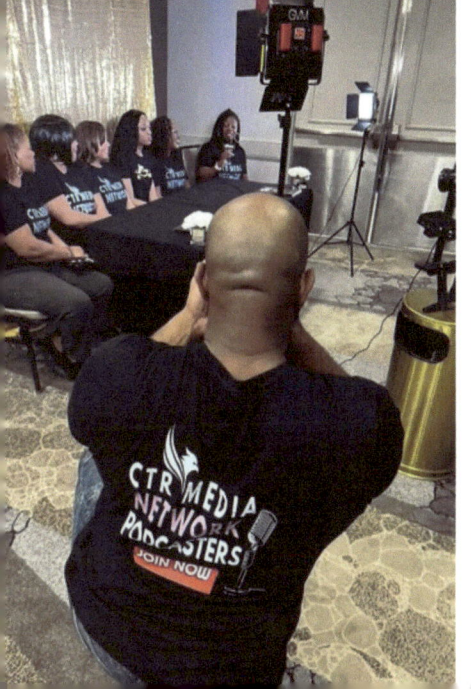

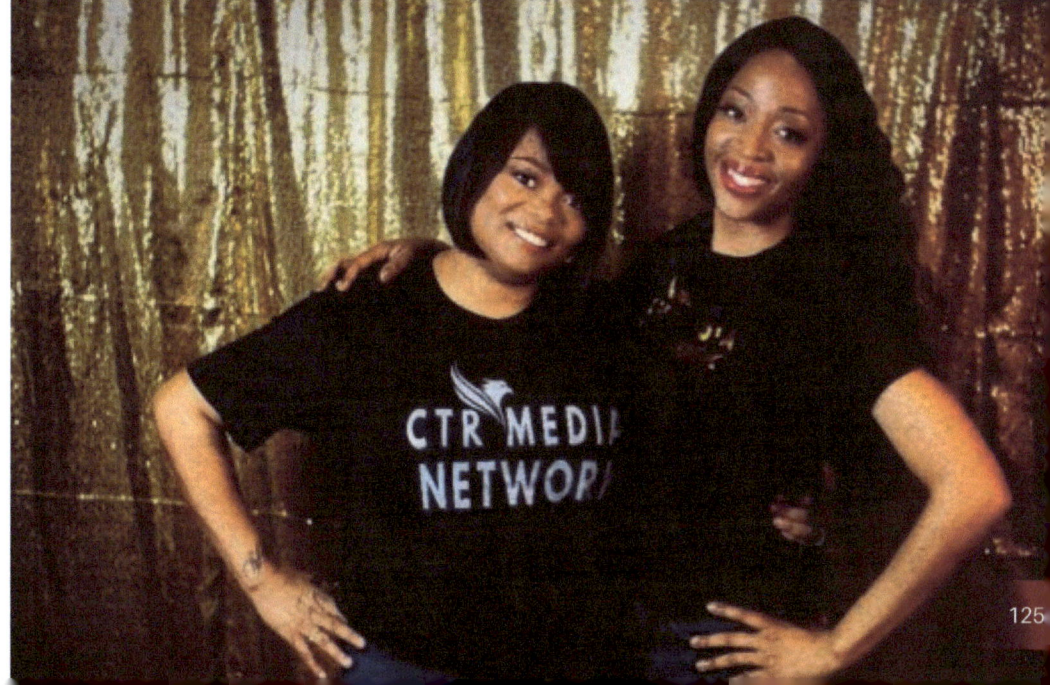

PODCAST DIRECTORY

1. The Tina Ramsay Show Hosted by Dr. Tina J Ramsay
2. S.H.E. TRUCKING PODCAST Hosted by Sharae Moore & Community
3. IMW- Ingeniously Made Whole Hosted by Briatanny Petty
4. Michael Finkley Show Hosted by Dr. Micheal Finkley
5. King Can Read Podcast Hosted by King (4 years old World's youngest podcaster)
6. The Vera Thomas Show Hosted by Vera Thomas
7. The Edu Station Podcast Hosted by Lashon Carter
8. Movement For Global Health Hosted by Dr. Mary Zennett
9. WISDOM TIPS with Dr. Connie Green
10. NONPROFIT CEO PODCAST Hosted by Tiffany D Bell & Community
11. Men Can't Always Be Wrong Podcast Hosted by MCABW CAST
12. The Geo Monroe Show & Podcast Hosted by GEO Monroe
13. Beauty for Ashes with Tracie
14. Thequeencandipodcast Hosted by Miniimah Muhammad
15. Broadcasting With Boss Ladi Star
16. Leveling Up The Podcast with Alethia Tucker
17. The Mothers Place with Coach Shana Asby
18. Hello World Talk Show with Joy World
19. Book Talks with Sandy
20. The Kim Jacobs Show
21. The Speak Eazy Hosted by Constance Woulard
22. HUSH No More Champions Hosted by Dr. Vanessa Dunn Guyton
23. Sweet Blessings Hosted by Anna L Brothers
24. The Homeschooling Interactive Magazine Podcast
25. Melanated Homeschooling Families Podcast

PODCAST DIRECTORY

1. The Marlene Saunders Show & Podcast
2. Men Thoughts Podcast
3. Hello Hello, Everybody Podcast
4. Redefining Education for Generation Z Podcast Hosted by Professor Dr.Shauli Mukherjee (INDIA)
5. Prison H.O.P.E. Initiative Hosted By Ivan Cameron (LIVE from Prison)
6. Secret Legal Codes Revealed TV & Podcast Hosted by Dr. Lydie
7. Hot Topics! Hosted by: Gabrielle Crichlow
8. Urban Counsel Hosted by: Ny McKinney
9. According to His Purpose-Hosted by: Nani Renee Buckner
10. Inspiring Nations with Sonja Keeve
11. Fearless And Bold- Hosted by Krwnd Sotto
12. Confident Woman Incubator PODCAST -Hosted by Dr. Doreen Lettsome Reid
13. Selfless Love Talk-Hosted by Chanel Budd
14. Convos With Anita Santiago
15. Chat And Chew w/Ms. Kecia-Hosted by LAKECIA GRIFFIN
16. Let's Talk About Healing- Hosted by Yvonne Pierre
17. Friends W/ Influence– Hosted by Elaundrea Akia
18. Enjoying Life OTR -Hosted by Cindy Tunstall
19. Spot light- Hosted by Iran (rain) Evans
20. Boss Confessions-Hosted by Ashauna Higgins
21. Conversationz with Friendz Hosted by Charlene Taylor
22. Leap Before You Look Podcast Hosted by Kyra Watson
23. The Private Room with Tiffany Hosted by Tiffany Brown
24. HealthDrips- Hosted by Paulishia Augillard
25. Childcare Pro Circle Hosted by Spring C Jackson

PODCAST DIRECTORY

1. **Westside Misfits Hosted by Donna Cameron**
2. **Fire Knowledge 4 Hustlers- Hosted by Author ChillFetti Chillfetti**
3. **Black regalia Podcast Hosted by Markel Jackson**
4. **Stories Dil se Hamesha-Hosted by Lata Giri**
5. **Misogynoir MurdersHosted by Ronnetta Rideout**
6. **From The Ashes Hosted by Ditra Graves**
7. **Black regalia Podcast Hosted by Markel Jackson**
8. **Inner Pieces Blog and Podcast Hosted by Alisa Esteves**
9. **Pearls & Politics Podcast Hosted by -Kahalah Clay**
10. **Cleverly Changing Podcast-Hosted by Elle Cole**
11. **Politics but make it Fashion Hosted by Amber Viola**
12. **Nun But Greatness- Hosted by Xavier Jones**
13. **StanTheMan Podcast**
14. **Thizcudbabook -Rochelle - Hosted by Fatimah Tisdale**
15. **The Pleasure's All Yours-Hosted by Lex Elia**
16. **Unapologetically Black: Never Broken. Always Empowered.-Hosted by Brittany Winfield**
17. **Warning Label Podcast- Hosted by Adrian Caruthers**
18. **The Unfiltered Point of View-Hosted by Derrick Braxton**
19. **Key to the City-Hosted by Keoni Gray**
20. **The Balancing Act- Hosted by E'Tiana Larkin**
21. **Da Urban Conservative -Hosted by Chaz Neal**
22. **Moms Who Achieve- Hosted bHosted by Regina Sloan**
23. **Daily Dose of Love with Tatia -Hosted by Tatia Bradley**
24. **Dearsis Podcast -Hosted by Myrtha Jasmin**
25. **Champagne And Sugar Cookies -Hosted by Raven Miller**

PODCAST DIRECTORY

1. **Girl, Goodnight -Hosted by LaKia McMillan**
2. **Adjusting Crowns The Podcast- Hosted by Sydney Symone**
3. **Morning Mimosas Hosted by -Holly Sisa**
4. **The Disruptive Entrepreneur by Rob Moore**
5. **Influential Entrepreneurs with Mike Saunders, MBA**
6. **Dave Lukas, The Misfit Entrepreneur_Breakthrough Entrepreneurship by Dave Lukas**
7. **Accountability On Demand (AOD) Podcast The Fighting Entrepreneur By Lashana West**
8. **Write About Now By Jonathan Small**
9. **The Bestseller Experiment By Mark Stay & Mark Desvaux**
10. **The Coaches Corner Claimed By Lucas Rubix**
11. **The Virtuous Coach Podcast By Cody Smith**
12. **Master Coach Collection By Gideon Culman**
13. **She Podcasts Elsie Escobar and Jessica Kupferman**
14. **Stark Reflections on Writing and Publishing By Mark Leslie Lefebvre**
15. **The Creative Penn Podcast For Writers By Joanna Penn**
16. **Write from the Deep By Karen Ball & Erin Taylor Young**
17. **Sage Family By Rachel Rainbolt**
18. **Step It Up Entrepreneur By Tomas Keenan**
19. **The Entrepreneur Experiment By Gary Fox**
20. **The 10 Minute Entrepreneur by Sean Castrina**
21. **The How-to Entrepreneur By Dylan Menter**
22. **The Sure Shot Entrepreneur by Gopi Rangan**
23. **Entrepreneur Motivation Podcast by Chris Bello**
24. **MissLiz Teatime**
25. **Daily Dose of Love with Tatia**

GRAB A MEMBERSHIP

POP UP AND CREATE

2100 SQ FT MULTI-PURPOSE CONTENT CREATION STUDIO

"FOUNDING 100" MEMBERSHIP $500 PER MONTH

- 2 hours per week Podcast Space ($500 value)
- 4 hour Large Event Space rental ($1000 value)
- Free Pop Up Monthly Events (Priceless)
- 2 Pop Up 1/2 Day Passes ($250 value)
- 2 Friend and Family 1/2 day Pass ($250 value)

Total value $2,000 +

PODCAST PRO $300 PER MONTH

- 2 hours per week Podcast Space ($500 value)
- Free Pop Up Monthly Events (Priceless)
- 2 Pop Up 1/2 Day Passes ($250 value)

Total Value $750 +

Mention CTR Media Network to receive a discount

CALL OR TEXT: 678-849-5813 TO LEARN MORE

@POPUPANDCREATE

WWW.POPUPANDCREATE.COM

2130 KINGSTON CT UNIT D MARIETTA GA 30067

POP UP AND CREATE

YOUR CREATIVE HOME

Build you confidence and community all in one place!

Book your next photoshoot, unique event, interactive activity and more with us!

- Entire 2100 sg ft Studio $300 per hour
- Content Suite $50 per hour
- Large Media event space $150 per hour
- Monthly Events $40
- Pop Up 1/2 Day Pass $150 (3-4 hours)
- Pop Up Day Pass $275 (6-8 hours)

Mention CTR Media Network to receive a discount

2130 Kingston CT Unit D Marietta GA 30067

678-849-5813 | www.popupandcreate.com | @popupandcreate

BLUEBUTTERFLYSKYE

MEET *Tina Haywood*

Bluebutterfly Skye

Additional Info

The BlueButterfly Represents Transformation on all levels Physical~ Self love , boundaries, renewal, declutter, nourishment. Spiritual~Soul connection Energetic~Circle of influence. Emotional ~Self Talk The ButterflySkye encourage you to flow through your own transformation to help you grow your confidence again and become a strong warrior.
Tina Haywood

Bluebutterfly Skye.com.au

Tina Haywood. She's a proud Yupungathi / Gangalidda woman, a descendant from ancestors who have walked this earth for 65,000 years. The spirit in her heart made her the strong woman that she is today. Tina is a survivor of Domestic Violence from living in poverty , with racism and discrimination throughout her journey and she is a strong leader as she is a mother, Author of "We are Warriors" , business owner and works in the Australian military, a woman who wears many hats . She have worked in many different areas & I'm passionate about helping youth, women and indigenous communities In Australia and globally my story is someone else survival guide .

Turning the roles from being a victim to becoming responsible for your personal happiness and re-writing your own story despite the challenges that life puts in your way is something not many people choose to do. It's not an easy option to choose, probably that's why. It takes courage, it takes realization, it may be painful and in the first place, it requires awareness - which can only be gained by focusing on what is inside yourself.

Tina Haywood is one of those fighters who overcame trauma and turned her suffering into power, resilience, and a mission:

"My goal is to help women escape domestic violence and sexual assault and to become strong, self-sufficient warriors who can return home and lead their communities into the future."

The mother who wears many hats, who is a mum, a business owner, a mentor, keynote speaker and a strong resilient leader is with her program called BluebutterflySkye - a transformational complete empowerment program that aims to promote the following rebirth, hope, and bravery for target audience impacted by Suicide, specifically aimed at Indigenous/ ATSI community, Youth and DV victims.

The symbolism of a butterfly is the foundation of BlueButterflySky which was chosen as "Butterflies show us how we can go within ourselves to dissolve old forms and morph, rebuilding and evolving ourselves," she explains, noting that they show us the importance of surrender and trust "as part of the essential process of growth and renewal."

https://bluebutterflyskye.com.au/about

Featured THE *Tina Ramsay* SHOW

CTR MEDIA
NETWORK
PODCASTERS

ROKU   SUBSCRIBE

CTRMediaNetwork.com

Download our CTRMN Channel on Roku TV and Watch our Podcast Shows for Free!

ADVERTISEMENT
ADS
with us!

TV

Watch our Podcasters on CTR Media Network Roku TV

PODCAST REVOLUTION MAGAZINE   134

On "Hot Topics!", we talk real talk about education, employment, health, or anything else steamy

Hosted by: Gabrielle Crichlow

The legal podcast !! From formal to informal hood politics, systematic oppression and everything in between ⚖️

Hosted by: Ny McKinney

A faith based podcast that focuses on healing, growing and discovering your God given purpose. We strive to help our listeners recognize issues that's stopping us from achieving our goals. We push courage, confidence and self love as our foundation to becoming the best version of ourselves

Hosted by: Nani Renee Buckner

Interviewing Women from across the globe that have stories of how they inspire others everyday.

Hosted by: Sonja Keeve

My Podcast Is Aimed At Casting A Spotlight On Artists Around Me That Have Inspired Me. And/Or Have A Positive & Uplifting Message. I Initially Began With Just Audio In 2022. But Have Recently Teamed Up With An Established & Talented Visual Creator From Connecticut. It Is My Intent To Show Support Solidarity & Overall United Front In Not Only The Creative World. But In Black/Latino World As A Whole.

Hosted by: Krwnd Sotto

Conversations with Danne

Coming Soon!

Confident Woman Incubator PODCAST Platform is for Confident Christian Woman Coaches & CEO's that desire to Unlock What's Inside You TM and learn how develop a Business BLUEPRINT; gain clarity on their specific Mission, Message, Mandate, Mantle to MARKETPLACE.

Hosted by: Dr. Doreen Lettsome Reid

Sharing the importance of loving yourselves and others more unselfishly. Communicating everyday challenges and encouraging others to heal, grow and support each other in this space.

Hosted by: Chanel Budd

No topic off limits. We share our experiences with you. .

Hosted by: LAKECIA GRIFFIN

Yvonne Pierre has conversations with guests on various topics on healing the mind, body, and spirit. Topics such as healing from childhood trauma, depression, burnout, hormonal health, and more.

Our podcast topics are limitless. We talk love, mental health, disappointment, success, and everything in between. We have created a space to be authentically ourselves vent and be vulnerable without judgement.

Hosted by: Elaundrea Akia

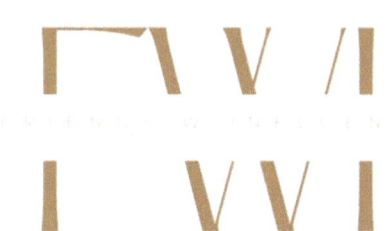

Enjoying Life OTR is a community that champions: adventure, innovation and well-being. We are sharing ways to stay connected, stay healthy and make the most of the opportunity to travel. We talk about the business and lifestyle of OTR trucking!

Hosted by: Cindy Tunstall

It's a platform for say what need to be said, actors ,musicians, people to promote.

Hosted by: Iran (rain) Evans

We offer a safe space for bosses to reveal their truth that will inspire early stage entrepreneurs to keep God first, to trust the process, to embrace failures and to never forget that all dreams are possible.

Hosted by: Ashauna Higgins

We cover various topics, we talk about it All. from Mental Health, Dating, Childhood Traumas to Politics

Hosted by: Charlene Taylor

We interview people who have something to say including controversial topics. We have a relationships and sex talk panel as well as an all male panel. We support artist and businesses through our spotlight moments on each episode. Adult content only.

Hosted by: Tiffany Brown

HealthDrips Podcast provides educational and motivational resources to frontline workers.

Hosted by: Paulishia Augillard

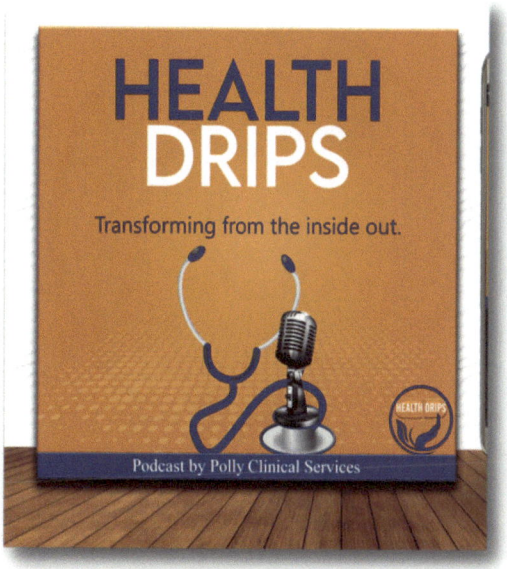

This podcast aims to help childcare professionals leverage information to create, scale, and grow their businesses. I am your host Spring C Jackson, childcare owner, your Winner Circle Childcare Consultant, best-selling author & speaker.

Hosted by: Spring C Jackson

FIRE KNOWLEDGE 4 HUSTLERS

I address universal Knowledge and give out true information which the most important commodity on this Planet.

Hosted by:Author ChillFetti Chillfetti

My podcast is the collection of beautiful stories, true success stories till fictional soulful stories...
In today's life so much of depression, my stories really feel good feeling to ny listeners and viewers, lets connect for some new creative stories del se hamesha...

Hosted by: Lata Giri

A true crime podcast that shines a light on the cases of missing and murdered Black women and girls.

Hosted by: Ronnetta Rideout

My podcast explores topics related to life, relationships, current events, culture, mental health and wellness, and more through rich and colorful discussions. Guest speakers drop in from time to time to spice up the conversations! Subscribe on Apple, Spotify, Google podcasts or wherever you get your podcasts

Hosted by: Anita Santiago

Educational/Motivational Podcast.

Hosted by: Ditra Graves

BRP is a multi-dimensional black male-lead platform in which the hosts discuss the world through their own perspectives as they grow learn and experience new things every week . It touches finance, health, religion, social, political issues, and definitely the culture !

Hosted by: Markel Jackson

Black Regalia Podcast

WestsideMisfits Radio Show is on Every Sunday at 3pm on our very own internet radio station.

Helping individuals understand how childhood trauma has affected the choices you have made as an adult. Sharing my experiences of childhood trauma, domestic violence, and other life experiences. To help others heal through their pain.

Hosted by: Talisa Esteves

Pearls & Politics Podcast is a platform for women and communities of color. Here at P&PP, we share pearls of wisdom and spread political information not MISinformation. Our objective is to help individuals, families and communities transition from surviving to thriving in every area of life.

Hosted by: Kahalah Clay

Hosts Elle and Miriam are two African American homeschooling moms embarking on a self-defining journey that is showered with self-determination. Listen in on conversations that will encourage you to be your authentic self, while uplifting your spirit and motivating your inherent potential. They're defining what culture is for their families and want you to do the same.

Politics but make it Fashion is a hilarious weekly podcast hosted by two lifelong best friends. One is a liberal and one's a conservative, come along as they chat about fashion, politics, pop culture, motherhood and more! Come chat with us.

Hosted by: Amber Viola

Zay and friends discussing everything up under the sun and beyond. Expect outta pocket topics, mad jokes and a lot of in sync laughing.

Hosted by: Xavier Jones

StanTheMan
Podcast
www.stanthemanpodcast.com

StanTheMan Podcast is a Business and Entrepreneurship podcast covering marketing and new topics of the day.

Your Podcast deserves a Home!
Join CTR Media Network Today!
Memberships start at $199 per month

We focus on topics that affect the black community, black mental health and the breaking down of generational curses an other taboo subjects.

Hosted by: Brittany Winfield

The show is a unfiltered discussion about navigating life as a millennial. Our generation is has went through and going through so much that our parents (as well as parents parents) never even fathomed. Warning Label is smart, funny,explicit, and real.

Hosted by: Adrian Caruthers

Just a few regular guys from Detroit, Mississippi, Indianapolis, Chicago, and Texas. We about fatherhood, our different upbringing, the black male experience, and everyday current events. Although this is "another male dominated podcast", we're fair, honest, making sure we're never too bias.

KEONI GRAY

Key to the City podcast honors those, both locally and nationwide, who go against the grain to chase their dreams or spread their message!! K2TC places a focus on the community of creatives involved in music, film, art, entrepreneurship, community leadership, and so much more! Key to the City is here to promote your works of art for the enjoyment of those that unapologetically applaud your wins, losses, and all the struggle in between. Let us honor the gift of YOU and celebrate your exclusive creations! Welcome to the City. YOU are the Key! Build Witcha Kinfolk!!

The Balancing Act will discuss the different hats I wear and how they impact my mental health, motherhood and marriage.

I'll also try mom hacks, discuss strategies to combat stress, and occasionally talk with other women who are doing it all, making it look effortless.

Hosted by: E'Tiana Larkin

Da urban conservative is all about the news on the streets, gun violence, crime, politics, and how we solve our communities most hardest issues
How can we change our communities for the better?
Let's get back to family, community, foundational roots

Hosted by: Chaz Neal

My podcast is for mothers that want to achieve specific goals and be elevated women, moms, and human beings. I'll share tools to understand how to manage our minds to get what we want, how conscious parenting will break generational cycles, and provide a safe learning environment for first generation change makers.
Hosted by: Regina Sloan

Dearsis is an invitation for conversation!

Hosted by: Myrtha Jasmin

We are 2 millennials who find the Funny in EVERYTHING! We giving y'all the Hood News , good topics , interviews and more every Monday and Friday

Binaural a beats and black voices combine to quiet your mind and relax you into your best night's sleep. Settle down and immerse yourself into original and classic stories with a melanated twist. In no time, you'll be "Sleeping in Melanated Peace." Girl, Goodnight

Hosted by: LaKia McMillan

Let's talk about the hurt, the pain, the frustration. Let's get to the root of our issues and then focus on the "release." Let's begin Adjusting Crowns.

Adjusting Crowns-The Podcast: A show made by a black queen, for all black queens.

Hosted by: Sydney Symone

We put value in criminal Justice promoting healing and education in the black community.

Hosted by: Holly Sisa

The Power Of Podcasting

Thank you to our Sponsors

SettleShark

HappyandHealthy.Global

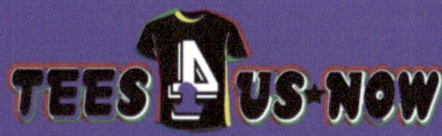

PODCAST REVOLUTION MAGAZINE

PODCAST REVOLUTION MAGAZINE

CTR MEDIA
NETWORK
PODCASTERS

CTRMediaNetwork.com

JOIN OUR FREE FACEBOOK COMMUNITY

SCAN ME

- Share your Podcast
- Business
- Services

PODCAST REVOLUTION MAGAZINE

PODCAST REVOLUTION Magazine

The Podcast Revolution Magazine is the first to educate, motivate, inspire, and address the complete needs of the Podcaster. Our Magazine provides insightful and informative coverage of the rapidly-evolving world of podcasting. Through in-depth articles, interviews, and analysis, the magazine offers readers a comprehensive interactive look at the latest trends, events, monetization tips, fascinating stories, technologies, and personalities shaping this dynamic industry. Could you share this with your family and friends?

We had a fantastic time with our event's guests, speakers, and sponsors. At our 1st **Power of Podcasting Event** in Georgia, we sold- out because of God and you. Thank you for your continued support. We celebrate alongside you our number one best-selling book, **The Power of Podcasting, available on Amazon.**

We are immensely grateful for every supporter, sponsor, affiliate, business owner, and podcaster who has invested in our platform, enabling us to improve and maintain our services continuously. To stay updated with our latest news and content, follow us on all our social media platforms and Roku TV at CTR Media Network. We are excited to announce our weekly **LIVE Power of Podcasting Class. To** join and learn more, **email us** at **ctrmedianetwork1@gmail.com.**

Your unwavering support inspires us to remain positive, motivated and focused on making a meaningful impact. We invite you to join us on this incredible journey of starting your podcast, and becoming a member of CTR Media Network where you can share your unique voice and make a difference in the world reaching 350 Million Households Worldwide. Together, let's create something extraordinary!

www.ingramcontent.com/pod-product-compliance
Lightning Source LLC
Chambersburg PA
CBHW041456280526
45792CB00004B/1034